Testament of
My
Childhood

*

ROBERT de ROQUEBRUNE

Translated by
FELIX WALTER

UNIVERSITY OF TORONTO PRESS

Original French edition published by
FIDES, 1958

English translation
© UNIVERSITY OF TORONTO PRESS 1964
Toronto and Buffalo

Reprinted 1972
Printed in the United States of America

ISBN 0-8020-6022-6
LC 64-4160

A JOSÉE
LA ROQUE DE ROQUEBRUNE

« Testament de mon enfance », c'est à Liszt, chère Josée, que j'ai emprunté ce titre, à Liszt qui a appelé l'une de ses premières œuvres « Testament de ma jeunesse ».

R.R.

Contents

✦

Part One

❋

THE MANOR-HOUSE

My childhood years in Canada were spent in a world that has vanished. Those years between 1890 and 1905 passed as if in a completely different universe—not only remote from us in time, but remote in the appearance of things, in the way people thought, and the way they acted. So entirely has the world of my childhood disappeared, so alien has it become, that I can scarcely even remember it.

Life as we lived it in those days doesn't exist any more. The break between then and now has been so complete, that even having known that era gives me the sensation of having lived on another planet.

Canada was quite a different sort of country then, with different customs and habits. When from the depths of my memory I recall those scenes from my childhood, I feel as if I were turning the leaves of some ancient manuscript which has been left lying in a drawer for half a century. The ink has faded, and the words are sometimes hard to decipher; whole passages remain unintelligible. But suddenly an entire page is lit up with such clarity, that what was almost obliterated takes shape once again, if only for a moment. For a brief instant, a dead life begins to throb within me, and I press my hand against my breast to still the beatings of my heart.

For it is a very moving experience to bring back to life a past age, and to resurrect those who are gone.

1

In our old house, surrounded by its gardens, we lived on a sort of island far from the rest of the world. We heard little of what went on outside. Some families do live like this, remote, self-sufficient, content with a garden, a wood, and a strip of river. They never seem to feel the need for broader horizons, where chance and adventure may lurk.

My father and mother had both preserved the attitudes of their youthful days. In them survived the remnants of a society which had been created by their parents and grandparents and which by this time had almost entirely disappeared.

Their attitude towards life caused them to live in a spiritual isolation which was as absolute as that of the house itself, surrounded by its trees, its flowerbeds, and its lawns.

In the midst of all this, we lived a profoundly peaceful, amazingly happy life. That big house, with its low-ceilinged rooms, its mahogany and velvet furniture, its black marble mantelpieces, and its oil lamps, was for years a really carefree home. The very fact that I was born into it predisposed me to happiness.

Indeed it is probably because of my birth in this house that I have always been passionately devoted to happiness. And if I have always sought it, always pursued it, it is because I once knew happiness and have since always tried to recapture it.

But each time I have thought it within my grasp, the memory of my childhood home has come back to me, and it seems to me that everything in my life which even resembles happiness has come to be associated with the place where I first encountered it.

These childhood years of mine seem to have lasted for a very long time. When I recall our life together in the manor-house, it seems quite endless, a sort of blissful eternity. It is as if my existence as a child had lasted through a whole normal lifetime. But then there was so much happening and so many people crowded into it! Besides, my emotions then were so sensitive and so fresh that everything impressed me deeply.

When I recall my childhood now with the eyes and the ears of memory, I relive forgotten vistas, forgotten echoes. And when this happens I am thrown back into a past that seems like something out of a fairy-tale.

I am aware that many men and women have completely lost their childhood. Or at best they have retained a colourless, shadowy recollection of that period, and hardly ever think of it. Such a surrender of childhood memories is a sure sign of indifference to oneself, but then lots of people are not really very interested in themselves. They easily forget their own pasts and are frankly bored with their own persons. Their lives are a day-to-day affair, and they let the past die out completely, as if there were nothing about it which made it worth holding on to, and yet the life of any individual may have its moments of poetry and passion. Childhood in particular is full of such moments.

The name "manor-house," which at the end of the nineteenth century was still used for the old seigneurial dwellings of French Canada, was far more imposing than the actual structures it designated.

The manor-house of Saint-Ours, at L'Assomption, came down to us from a great-grand-aunt on my mother's side. My mother was brought up in it and it was from there that she was married. We were all born there too.

It stood about two miles from the village, on the highway to Montreal. It was a big stone house, with a long roof pierced by dormer windows. The entrance was framed by a wooden porch with a flight of stone steps leading up to it. This porch was right at one end of the house, and there were five windows along the front. The big roof with its five dormer windows put the finishing touches to a building that was simple, perhaps, but harmonious. Two chimneys topped the roof at either end. Along the back of the house ran a long wooden veranda.

From the end of the seventeenth century down to our own time this manor-house had been lived in by a good many people and, through inheritance and relationships, had passed from the Le Gardeurs to the Saint-Ours and from them to my mother. In 1790 it had been partly rebuilt by our great-grand-uncle, Charles Auguste d'Eschaillon de Saint-Ours.

His portrait hung in the dining-room to the right of the fireplace. It showed a young man with white hair, and for a long time this completely puzzled me. But one day my mother told me that in the days when Saint-Ours was a young man it was the fashion for people to wear powder in their hair, and so the mystery was solved.

My great-grand-aunt's portrait also hung in the dining-room and formed a companion-piece to her husband's. It had been painted by Hamel and showed an old lady in a black lace bonnet. It was hard for me to understand how this elderly person could have been married to the young man on the other side of the marble chimney-piece. Then one day I learned that Uncle Saint-Ours had had his portrait painted in his youth and our aunt had had hers done when she was quite old, and that explained the difference in age between the two. This was my first encounter with the gap between generations and with the flight of time, and it was in this way that I had my first lesson on the nature of life and the presence of death.

Charles Auguste d'Eschaillon, Chevalier de Saint-Ours, died in 1837, and his widow married again in 1843. Her second husband was Louis Michel Viger, the man who was always called "the President" because he was President of the Peoples' Bank in Montreal. He was both a banker and a politician; he sat for Terrebonne and, in 1848, was made Receiver General. Of the four Vigers, this is the one as well who was always referred to as "le beau Viger." The others were Denis Benjamin Viger, member of the Legislative Council, Jacques Viger, mayor of Montreal, and Bonaventure Viger, rebel of 1837 who, after fleeing with La Roque de Roquebrune and Lambert, was taken prisoner at the border and sentenced to be transported. These Vigers were a wealthy family. The mayor of Montreal gave his name to Viger Square. He married the last of the La Cornes, a daughter of the Chevalier de La Corne-Saint-Luc who was also the widow of Lord Lennox.

Saint-Luc was seigneur of L'Assomption and Viger was seigneur of Repentigny. Their widow inherited from both her husbands, and people in that part of the country always called her "the seigneuresse." She was a rich woman for those days and, as she had no children, she decided to make a home for her grand-niece, Anne Lilia d'Irumberry de Salaberry, who was my mother, and who was only five years old when in 1857 she went to live in the manor-house. When I was born there, the old house had not been altered since the days of Uncle Saint-Ours.

The Chevalier had been an odd sort of man, and some of his manias had become family legends.

He had a horror of metal, of any kind of metal. The least contact with it was most disagreeable to him. For this reason he would never handle coins. When he went shopping in Montreal, he was always accompanied by a servant with a leather purse. When it came time to settle up, Saint-Ours would simply turn to the servant and say: "Baptiste, please pay." And Baptiste would pay. Because of this phobia, Uncle Saint-Ours never opened a door or pulled out a drawer; a servant would always have to do it for him. At table, he used cutlery stamped with his arms, which were a bear passant on a field sable, but he always wore gloves. Throughout his life he took all his meals with his gloves on.

The drawing-room in the manor-house was filled with mahogany furniture. There were great, well-stuffed arm-chairs, their wood carved with roses in full bloom, their upholstery of red velvet. There were also card-tables and what-nots. Two huge, high-backed sofas stood at one end, on either side of the door. In front of the black marble fireplace there was a round table with an epergne.

This was a strange and complicated object. It consisted of a silver base supporting a number of glass vessels. I never knew what it was supposed to be used for nor did anybody else. I am inclined to think now that it served no useful purpose at all. It was an "ornament." This showy piece struck me as a very handsome object indeed. Thus, at a very tender age, I showed a taste for useless ostentation and for the poetry of decoration.

The what-nots—there were two of them—lent an odd note to the room because of their shape. They were made of black walnut and had a typical Victorian ugliness. They dated from the time of my parents' marriage in 1874. A "what-not" was a sort of table supporting a mirror, which was surrounded by little shelves of different sizes, the ones on top smaller than the ones below. On this curious monument it was customary to display bric-à-brac—objects in porcelain or bronze, which represented a stag running, a cat in a slipper, or a lady of olden times (but of what times? for the fashions were a little vague), and other articles of similar taste. There was also a Meissen china bouquet whose flowers were so fresh and bright that they rivalled the real flowers from our garden which my mother used to set out on the mantelpiece in summertime.

The pictures in the drawing-room were hung from thick cords of red silk, and to make them easier to see they were made to stick out from the wall at a sharp angle. This was done by means of a wedge fastened at the back.

A child is always likely to be affected by the contents of the house where sensibility first comes to him, but nothing makes so deep an impression as pictures, engravings, and portraits.

There were a number of hunting scenes on the walls of the drawing-room: a stag at bay, dying, with the pack in a circle about him; a young lady in a riding-habit giving a lump of sugar to her mount.

One engraving represented "A Winter Scene in Holland": there was an ice-covered canal, skaters, a windmill. But all this left me quite unmoved; indeed I found it rather boring. After all, I saw dogs and horses every day, in the fields, on the road, or out in front of the house. A lady on horseback was hardly a marvel to a child who had often seen his mother dressed in a riding-habit alight at the front door. As for the stag and the winter scene, these were just transpositions of reality, for the winter scene did nothing to stimulate my imagination. The fact that it was supposed to be in Holland was of no consequence to the little boy who looked at it, because I didn't know what Holland was, but I was perfectly familiar with snow and ice and sleighs and skaters. There weren't any windmills at L'Assomption or at St. Sulpice or at Repentigny, but this minor point didn't bother me, and for a long time I was convinced that this picture was a picture of skaters I had often seen in winter on the little river behind our house. I wasn't very exacting on the subject of realism in art.

In just the same way the death of the stag seemed to me to represent what probably happened out in the woods when my father or Jacques came back with fresh venison.

But there were two large coloured engravings which did give me food for thought. Through them I penetrated an unknown world. One showed a young woman and a young man in a carriage drawn by galloping horses. In the background was a mountain landscape. It was a picture full of drama. The young woman's head rested on the young man's breast, and he was busy kissing her and driving his horses at one and the same time. I found this complicated situation very stimulating. Beneath the picture was a single word in English: "Elopement." One day I asked Roquebrune, my brother, what this word meant and, as he knew a little English, he told me. As a matter of fact I wasn't greatly surprised to learn that the picture was called "Elopement," as I had been quite able to follow the artist's intentions. These two young people had obviously been crossed in love and had had to flee to overcome the obstacles to their happiness. For a very long time this picture was to me the epitome of love, and, if I have never been able to think of love except in terms of drama and of conquest, it is perhaps because of this picture that I looked at so often, this picture of a young man and a young woman dashing along a mountain road behind two galloping horses.

Another "picture" in the drawing-room had the same power to put me into a state of reverie. This one showed a large ship about to set sail from a quay strewn with barrels and bales and coils of rope. A knot of people were waving their handkerchiefs in farewell to a man and a woman standing on the deck. In the background were huge waves breaking. Soon this big ship would be dancing from crest to crest like those others one could see out in the open heeled over to the wind. This picture also bore a title printed on the frame below. It was called "The Farewell," and to me this was the sequel to the romance begun in the other picture. Though these two works had no connection with one another, I associated them in my mind as two acts in a single drama.

Many years later, neither the Louvre in Paris nor the National Gallery in London nor the Academia in Venice was ever to give me as much pleasure as these two romantic engravings. No, no museum in all Europe, no exhibition of world-famous pictures, has made me feel as deeply as those two naïve pictures hanging in the drawing-room of the house where I grew up.

The walls of the dining-room were peopled, too, with a number of motionless figures. This silent, solemn company filled me with a secret terror. The subjects themselves overawed me and I was quite bewildered by the costumes in which these people were dressed. I was very astonished to learn that these were my father's grandparents and great-grandparents. The portraits had been painted at different periods and some of the artists were obviously more gifted than others. The subject of the most ancient of them all was a solemn-faced man wearing a bob wig. Both the colour and the cut of his coat had faded out into the shadowy background, but his lace jabot and cuffs still gleamed with a pale white light. All one could really discern was a head framed by powdered hair, and the lace at the neck and at the cuffs of the coat. This was my father's great-great-grandfather. His disembodied head, standing out from the canvas in sharp relief, looked like a ghost, and the odd-looking old gentleman was no favourite of mine.

I was much fonder of a young woman in a peaked bonnet, whose picture hung on the wall not far from the forbidding great-great-grandfather. She had posed seated and was wearing a panniered dress, which billowed out around her and was cut off short by the gilt line of the frame. Her silken dress was a delightful shade of old rose and its flowered pattern could be made out quite clearly. In one hand she held a book with a red binding, and she had one finger between the leaves marking her place. Her other hand rested in her lap, and there was a generous display of bosom partly veiled by a fichu of fine lawn. Round her slender, well-modelled neck was fastened a very narrow black silk ribbon. The rather sad look in her eyes together with the smile on her lips gave her a charmingly enigmatic expression. I always felt especially friendly towards her. Once, years later, I saw this picture again in my brother René's house, and I remember giving an affectionate nod to the ancestress with the flowered dress.

The dining-room was much more comfortable than the drawing-room, so we spent a good deal of time in it. I can really remember it best as it was in autumn with the logs blazing in the fireplace, or in winter with the big stove growling away in one corner. Here in the evenings I had a chance to see my parents. My father would sit and read in his big arm-chair not far from the fire, and it could never get too hot for him. My mother would do her sewing or her darning near a little table, which held a lamp, her sewing-basket, and a book or two. There would be long silences interrupted from time to time by animated snatches of talk, and all this while I played about on the carpet at their feet.

Nothing that was said in the course of those long winter evenings is of much importance today. The words uttered in that spacious room have evaporated and melted away, have been carried off like wisps of smoke in the wind. All that remains in my memory is an indistinct and gentle murmur of voices. Sometimes my mother's silvery laugh would ring out across the room. Then my brothers, sitting around the big table with their school-books, would look up suddenly. My father would lower his voice again, and whatever it was he was saying seemed to amuse my mother considerably because she would lean towards him with a happy smile.

But I do recall a single remark made one evening in that room, a remark full of mystery and the unknown. My parents had been sitting together for some time without saying a word; in fact their silence had been unusually protracted. My mother looked preoccupied and perhaps a trifle sad. My father, seated in his big arm-chair, held a book in his hands, but I knew he wasn't reading. He kept glancing about the room absent-mindedly and staring into the dark corners. Then Mother looked up from her work and their eyes met.

"It'll be tomorrow," he said.

My mother seemed very much affected by this remark. For a time she sat quite still with her hands clasped in her lap, and when she took up her sewing again she seemed to be trembling a little.

Later, years later, I questioned her about this occurrence, which I had never forgotten. She seemed surprised and couldn't remember anything about it. So it would seem that people can completely forget moments of unhappiness in their own past lives. Whatever it was that was to happen next day, and which made my mother so anxious at the time, had been completely effaced from her memory.

Sambo came to the house before I did. I mean to say he was already living there before I was born, so when I opened my eyes for the first time, the old negro was a well-established member of the household. This gave him the right later on, whenever he had trouble with me, or I was about to do something naughty, to say in a tone of authority, "I done go to the village to fetch Dr. Forêt when you was borned; I done hold you when you wasn't more than five minutes old." This was his way of making me aware of the difference between a man of his age and a mere boy.

The old negro had turned up one evening about Christmas-time, like one of the Wise Men of the East who had lost his way in the snow. I have often heard the story of how he arrived. He knocked at the kitchen door and Sophronie opened it. Sambo said, "Ma'am, this poor nigger ain't had nothing to eat and he's mighty cold." And big Sophronie led him at once into the kitchen where she was getting dinner ready. Sambo was given a place beside Godefroy and had something to eat. Then Mother came into the kitchen, then my father, then Roquebrune and my sisters. Each time someone came in, Sambo repeated, "This poor nigger ain't had nothing to eat and he's mighty cold." They all nodded sympathetically, because it was terribly cold outdoors. Sambo was given a place to sleep for the night on the upper floor of the shed behind the house. Godefroy had his living-quarters there, and the place was heated by a big stove. Next day the negro didn't say anything about leaving, so nobody else mentioned anything to him about it either.

And Sambo never did leave.

All this happened in a perfectly straightforward way, because, as a matter of fact, Sambo and big Sophronie and my father and mother too were quite simple people, genuinely human and in every way worthy of one another. Nobody ever asked Sambo any personal questions. In course of time, though, he did in his halting French manage to talk occasionally about his earlier life. We learned that he had been a slave in Virginia in his younger days, before the Civil War. Then he had been in service in Boston, but that hadn't been much of a change. He went to Montreal with his employers and had been on his way to a factory in Joliette when fate, on a December evening, brought him to our door.

My parents believed that Sambo had been sent by God, and Sambo too thought that God had guided him to their house. They were none of them so far wrong, because, as a matter of fact, neither Sambo nor my parents ever had a moment's cause to regret his coming.

Sambo was just as deeply religious as my father and mother. He was a Methodist, and among his belongings he had a big English Bible in the King James version, which he pored over laboriously but diligently every Sunday. His chief job at the manor-house was to act as coachman, and he used to drive the family into the village of L'Assomption to attend Mass. This was destined to influence his spiritual life. After he had hitched the horse to the cross-bar in front of the church steps, he used to stand just inside the door, drawn there, it seemed, by the sermons of the parish priest, the Abbé Dorval. His sermons seemed to entrance Sambo. The old negro spoke French very badly to the end of his days, but he soon managed to understand it well enough, and he found the Abbé Dorval's eloquence profoundly moving.

Sambo was probably just about the only human on earth who ever thought that the Abbé Dorval was a great orator, for in the whole village of L'Assomption, and away beyond it as far as the seventh concession, there was general agreement on two points: that the Abbé Dorval was a saint of a man and that his sermons were unutterably dreary. The sermons that Jacques-Bénigne Bossuet preached before Louis XIV in the chapel of Versailles were perhaps finer than the humble homilies delivered by the Abbé Dorval in the village church of L'Assomption in the presence of Sambo, but what soul was ever really touched by the consummate art of the Bishop of Meaux? The King listened to Bossuet's high-flown periods and then went off to sleep with Madame de Montespan, but Sambo was so deeply affected by the words of the country priest that one day he announced his intention of abjuring his Methodist heresy. He was baptized into the Roman Catholic Church. My father and mother acted as his godparents, and Father Dorval had the joy of administering the sacrament of baptism to a neophyte who was really pure in heart.

This old black comrade of my childhood days has been dead for many years. He stayed on with us to the end, and my parents nursed him in his last illness. When he died he was holding their hands in his own wrinkled black hands with their pink palms. It seemed as if the death of the old negro marked the beginning of a period of worry and trouble for my parents, because very soon afterwards they encountered all sorts of financial adversities and had a very difficult time. They endured it all, however, with unfaltering courage and dignity, and finally won through to better days, but we always looked back on the years when Sambo was with us as the happiest of all those we spent in the manor-house. So, gradually, his name came to be linked in our minds with a whole epoch of unruffled prosperity and quiet content.

I have had a number of faithful accounts of what took place on the day I was born. Both Sophronie and Sambo often used to talk to me of the events of July 28. Indeed I've heard all about my arrival into this world and the first hours of my existence on so many occasions that it's almost as if I could remember it clearly myself. . . .

It was very hot. In Canada, in July, the sun blazes down, and that day the heat had been overpowering. But towards evening a faint breeze stirred in the garden. It brought the tang of the river and the fragrance of flowers into the house and it began to cool. Sophronie went around opening all the shutters. She noticed my mother coming in from the garden, leaning heavily on my father's arm. My parents had spent the afternoon together under the wooden parasol, over in the corner near the cedar hedge.

Mother seemed to be in pain, and Sophronie heard her say to my father, "It's time to go and get Dr. Forêt." A few minutes later Sambo drove off towards the village with the carriage.

Sophronie had all sorts of things to attend to in the kitchen. The birth of a child called for the cooking of head-cheese and the baking of cakes and pies. There were hams to cook, too, and joints of pork. There would be relatives staying in the house and a big spread on the day of the christening. Sophronie had had plenty of experience because there had already been eight children. This was to be the ninth.

In her fifteen years of married life my mother had had first two daughters and then six sons. Three of the boys had died. What was the next child going to be—a boy or a girl? Out in the kitchen there was much speculation on that point. Later, Sambo always claimed that he had said it was going to be a boy and that that boy was going to be me. But Sambo had a habit of mixing up his recollections and his prophecies. According to Sophronie's version, it was Old Mother Corbeille who was the first to tell my mother that she was going to have a son. "Madame is carrying her child very high," she said, "and it's a well-known fact that when a child lies near its mother's heart like that it's always a boy." Nobody could resist so scientific an observation, so they were not surprised out in the kitchen when my father came to tell them that I had just been born and that Old Mother Corbeille's services were required in my mother's bedroom.

Old Mother Corbeille was a woman of some experience. She was always called to the manor-house when a child was expected, though actually her services were limited to washing the new-born baby, rocking it to sleep, and keeping her eye on it at night. She wasn't in any sense of the word a wet-nurse. As a matter of fact, there weren't any in French Canada. My mother nursed all her children herself, and I fed from the same generous breast that had nourished all my brothers and sisters before me.

Mother told me once that my birth had been the easiest she had ever experienced, and that I had come into the world without hurting her. I wonder if that is why she was always so tender towards me, even when I had grown into a long-legged youth with a moustache just beginning to sprout. But then I was her youngest child, her last, and this too might explain her special fondness for me, a fondness which she never tried to hide, and which was in any case taken in good part by all the other members of the family.

When Old Mother Corbeille had made me presentable, she laid me in the cradle waiting for me in the room next to my mother's. Dr. Forêt and my father stayed on in my mother's room beside the bed where she was resting. In Canada, in those days, there was no question of deadening the pain for women in childbirth or of helping them through their agony by administering any sort of anaesthetic. The nuns of the Convent of the Sisters of Providence were told what was happening and said a prayer "with a special intention," while the Mother Superior sent Mamma a mysterious "girdle of St. Margaret." That was all the sufferer could expect to ease her pain. What was of most help to her, at the height of her agony, was the presence of her beloved husband, who stayed beside her holding her hand and whispering words of encouragement. As a matter of fact, this courageous woman had little need of support. She armed herself with her own will-power to face the ordeal she had undergone so many times before, and once the awful hours were over she relaxed in her bed, which had again become a bed of rest.

It was at that moment that my brothers and sisters were allowed in to see me and to make my acquaintance.

I probably looked a hideous little object, but the whole family went into raptures and said I was beautiful. Roquebrune took me in his arms to show me off to the others, and I chose that precise moment to make my voice heard for the first time. I started to cry, "just like an angry little kitten," as my eldest brother described it on one occasion when he was telling me of our first encounter. He got rid of me by passing me over to Big Sophronie.

The two Sophronies, Godefroy, and Sambo had joined the others in the bedroom by now, and it appears that I stopped crying as soon as Sophronie held me in her arms. She rocked me to and fro and I soon fell asleep in a refuge that I felt by instinct was a sure one. Such was the beginning, in the very first hour of my life, of the close understanding that was to develop between us.

The old Negro came over and wanted to hold me too, but Sophronie wouldn't let him. She laid me gently in my cradle without waking me up. Sambo came and leaned over me as I slept and, as he gently ran his big fingers over my forehead, he muttered mysterious sentences under his breath. Sophronie wanted to shoo him away, as she was afraid he would wake me up. Though the Negro stepped back a little, he now began to croon a sort of religious incantation in a low voice and made passes in the air.

Finally Big Sophronie dragged him out of the room by the arm, but I still slept on. If the Negro's signs and spells had any magic power, their mystic emanations passed into me without disturbing my sleep. But Big Sophronie was very annoyed. She was cross with Sambo for having cast his heathen spells over a new-born infant who hadn't yet been christened. When she told me all about it much later, I could see that Sophronie's Christian soul must have shuddered at its contact with black Sambo's idolatries. She had been afraid they might have some bad influence on the child to whom she was already passionately devoted. As soon as they got back to the kitchen she scolded Sambo roundly. But he didn't seem to mind, and explained that the words he had muttered and the tunes he had chanted were meant to bring me luck. Back in Virginia they always did that when a child was born. His fingers moving over my face had just been warding off evil spirits.

Old Mother Corbeille heard all this argument because Sophronie had dished out a substantial meal for her at one end of the huge kitchen table. Old Mother Corbeille was a great eater, so she was in Sophronie's good books, because Sophronie liked everybody around her to eat heartily. Old Mother Corbeille joined in the discussion while she munched her pie and gulped down her coffee. Her views were based on a wide experience of human destinies, and to her way of thinking the new baby, sleeping in his cradle, had absolutely nothing to worry about. It appeared I had been born under particularly happy auspices because I was the seventh in an unbroken line of sons. This was bound to bring me all sorts of luck and good fortune in later life. She even went so far as to assert that being a seventh son meant that a special gift had been conferred on me.

A gift! But what sort of a gift? Old Mother Corbeille's prophecies were never very clearly stated and the nature of the gift remained pretty vague. All through the years of my childhood I heard people talking about the gift I was supposed to possess, being a seventh son. My family felt there must be something in what the old woman said, and Mother and Hervé in particular were for a long time quite certain that this gift of fate actually existed. Their lively imaginations and their affection for me conjured up all sorts of qualities and graces, but it was never very clear in just what way I was supposed to be gifted. Yet when my mother held me in her lap she would often talk about it. "You are my seventh son," she would say, and she would gaze deep into my eyes to try and unravel the mystery. Often Hervé, when he and I were playing, would examine the palm of my hand carefully and say in a mysterious voice, "The gift must be written there." And he would slowly trace out the lines of my hand with his finger.

The day after I was born the first batch of relatives arrived by train, and the house became even more noisy and animated than usual. At no time did it ever seem sad or empty, but christenings filled it with a special gaiety. Then the old manor-house, that had belonged to the Saint-Ours and the Le Gardeurs, took on a new lease of life. Little Sophronie got all the spare rooms ready for their occupants. Some guests were bound to be staying on for a week or two afterwards. Everything had to be put in order for visits of this sort. French-Canadian hospitality at the end of the nineteenth century was still quite unsophisticated. It was understood that you could go and visit relatives and friends and stay with them for weeks on end without disturbing them. Little Sophronie made up the beds, filled the jugs with water, laid out towels on the washstands, and, as she was the chamber-maid, put the appropriately named pot into each commode. In addition to her usual duties she had been told by my father to make up two beds in the room Uncle Rouville was to occupy. This had meant fetching an iron bedstead down from the attic and setting it up beside the big four-poster. The fact was that Monsieur Hertel de Rouville and his wife were both expected.

Our Aunt Rouville was perfectly delightful to everybody except her husband. My father was very fond of his uncle, who happened to be the only close relative of that generation still living, and he was also very fond of Madame de Rouville, who was witty and charming and had a beautiful voice. Later, when I got to know my Aunt Rouville, I in my turn fell under the spell of that voice. It had a silvery timbre, which I found quite enchanting. No doubt it had been one of the things that had made my great-uncle fall in love with her. How could he fail to marry such a woman? And what had happened to the Rouvilles then to change their love to hate? Neither I nor any other member of the family ever found out. My father kept silent on that point, but what was common knowledge was that Monsieur and Madame de Rouville hadn't spoken to one another for years. As they were both very devout Catholics, there could be no question even of a separation, so they went on living together without ever speaking or even so much as looking at one another. They lived like that for years and years until death dissolved the marriage. When I was old enough to find out about this extraordinary situation, my uncle and aunt hadn't exchanged a single word for all of three decades.

It was my father himself who told me one day how his attempt to bring them together had failed completely. The idea of getting them to sleep in the same room had been his, and anyone who knew my father would have found the notion a characteristic one. He was quite convinced that no two people could spend a night in the same room together and still keep up a quarrel so futile that it was only kept going by silence on both sides. It was just the sort of idea a perfectly normal, healthy man would get into his head, but the Rouvilles seem to have been rather more complicated than their nephew. The night they spent in the same room did nothing to bring them together.

"You know," said my father years later, as he tugged at the points of his moustache, "you know, I made a mistake in putting that little iron bed alongside the big one. I ought to have got them to sleep in the same bed. No matter how big it is, a bed will bring a man and woman together again quicker than anything. I didn't go about it at all the right way. Now, if I ever get another chance. . . ."

But he never did, because, though Uncle and Aunt Rouville often came back to the manor-house, they always came singly. They must have been wary of fresh attempts at reconciliation, and their memory of the one made at the time I was christened must have been particularly disagreeable.

Other relatives and friends occupied the remaining rooms. Little Sophronie had more than one iron bedstead to set up. There were five or six of them kept in reserve in the attic. All the towels and bed linen stored there was used up too.

The moment she arrived, Grandmother Salaberry took charge of the table arrangements and the menu. The christening luncheon became her personal responsibility. She loved pottering about in the kitchen. When it came to planning the meals on an occasion such as this, she was in her element. She went about opening and shutting oven doors, helping Big Sophronie, keeping an eye on food cooking on the stove, beating eggs, and adding sugar to the desserts. Her hat and gloves were off in no time and she was busy laying the table.

Cousin Annie, who was a rather lazy girl, did nothing at all but wander about in the garden, for she loved flowers. She picked all the prettiest ones to make a bouquet for my godmother. Annie made it up of what we used to call "repeater" roses because they bloomed in June, as all roses do, and then again from the end of July until well into September. I got all these details about the bouquet from my godmother herself, as well as many other details about the events of my christening day. My godmother is quite an old lady now, but I see her often because she lives in Paris. It isn't so very far from the Avenue Hoche, where she lives, to my own house in Auteuil. And if the distance between us is scant, the same can be said of the gap between our ages, for she is only fourteen years older than I am. The person who sponsored me at that time-honoured religious ceremony was quite a little girl.

And my godfather was my eldest brother Roquebrune, who was a little boy of ten at the time.

My parents had so many children that all the uncles and aunts and not-too-distant cousins had had their turn at standing as godparents.

When I was born, it was decided that Roquebrune and my aunt, Thérèse de Salaberry, would "officiate," as the saying went in French Canada in those days. My mother's young sister lived at Chambly in the home of my grandmother Grosbois. Thérèse de Salaberry had been more or less adopted by Madame Grosbois when the colonel died at my parents' manor-house in 1880. So the child went to live in this little town where the hundred-year-old house of the Irumberrys with its colonnaded portico still stood in its own grounds, not far from the British barracks. Every day the little girl could see off in the distance the bastions and walls of Fort Pontchartrain, the expanse of water in Chambly Basin, and Belœil Mountain. It was a soft, sentimental landscape like a water-colour. But the little girl used to get rather bored living with her grandmother, and she often used to ask to go and stay with my parents where things were livelier. Then Madame de Grosbois would pack a bag with dresses and underthings and take the child to the Richelieu Navigation Wharf. There was a steamer for Montreal once or twice a week. Thérèse de Salaberry often made the trip, so everybody on board knew who she was and there was always somebody to take care of her. A few hours later the steamer would put in at St. Sulpice where my father would be waiting with a carriage for his young sister-in-law.

On maps of the province of Quebec the name Chambly appears not far from the name Champlain. Place-names in French Canada are often the names of people. Explorers, officers, colonists, and seigneurs have left their mark on the towns and lakes and rivers of Canada. Samuel de Champlain left his name to the huge lake he discovered in Louis XIII's day. The surname of Jacques de Chambly is perpetuated by the little town of which he was governor in the reign of Louis XIV. Along the St. Lawrence you find towns and villages bearing the names of Monsieur de Sorel, of Monsieur de Contrecœur, and of Monsieur de Verchères. Sorel, Verchères, and Contrecœur were officers of the Régiment de Carignan before they ever became place-names. Even the rivers are sometimes called after actual people, like the Richelieu named in honour of the cardinal.

To travel from Chambly to St. Sulpice, Thérèse de Salaberry went down the Richelieu and sailed past the town of Sorel and the villages of Verchères and Contrecœur. She didn't have to go on as far as Montreal. The big paddle-wheeler unloaded its boxes and bales and a few passengers on the wharf at St. Sulpice. That's where Thérèse de Salaberry came ashore on July 29, 1889. She saw the carriage on the road waiting for her with Sambo at the horse's head keeping a firm hold on the bridle because Jess always shied at steam whistles and reared and kicked in the shafts. Then a little boy came racing up to her with a big bunch of roses. He threw her arms round the little girl and shouted, "Our godchild is a boy and we're going to call him Robert." Then my godfather gave my godmother a big kiss.

They were waiting dinner for Thérèse in the manor-house and were all in the dining-room when she arrived. As she was the godmother, the little girl had the place of honour on my father's right, while the young godfather, Roquebrune, sat proudly at the right of Grandmother Salaberry.

Roquebrune was christened Paul, but by a sort of right of primogeniture he was always called Roquebrune by all the members of the family. This name of an old ancestral estate seemed to belong to him more than to any of the others as he was the eldest son. It was the last vestige of a feudal tradition which gave him by custom this courtesy title. We, his younger brothers, have always called him Roquebrune, and he has always signed his letters in that way without any Christian name. That had been the custom of the La Roques years ago in Gascony, and the Canadian La Roques had retained this special deference towards the eldest son. He has never been Paul to any of us but only Roquebrune. Even my father and mother always called him that, and later on, when he got married, so did his wife. French Canadians tend to preserve their old customs in this way and to hand them on from generation to generation. And this not only happens in families that take a pride in their military ancestry, or in vanished titles and seigneurial possessions, but also among those of bourgeois and peasant stock. Everybody in the province of Quebec has some sort of family tree and keeps a copy of it at home among his possessions. French Canadians know who their first Canadian ancestor was and from what French province and even from what French village he came. Go into an habitant's "parlour" or a city-dweller's drawing-room and you will see a big book lying on the table in the place of honour; it's the family history. Like the Rohans and the Montmorencys, the humblest French-Canadian farmers know who their ancestors were.

The fact is that French Canadians are proud of their French blood and of the ancient lineage from which they spring. A French Canadian called Jean Baptiste Sans-Quartier boasted on one occasion,

"We, Sir, were sent out to Canada by His Majesty King Louis XIV."
And Jean Baptiste Sans-Quartier was right, for he was descended
from a soldier who served in the Régiment de Chambellé, which was
dispatched to New France by the King, and his war-like, heroic
name is a reminder that the old royal colony was settled by soldiers.

During the luncheon there was a discussion about the name I was
to be given at my christening. The little baby still asleep upstairs had
no name as yet. Everybody had their own suggestions to offer.

But Roquebrune, who was, after all, to be godfather, used his
authority to settle the argument. "He's to be called Robert," he said.
And he added, "That's the name Mother wants."

The carriages drew up beside the porch steps. As this was an occasion,
they had all been pressed into service. Thérèse de Salaberry and
Roquebrune took their places in the big Berlin, which people called
a "rockway." Sambo was on the box and kept a tight rein on Tiger
and Jess who were in double harness. My father was to drive the
second carriage bringing my grandmother and the Rouvilles. Bob
was harnessed to this one. The third, with our old mare Fanny between the shafts and Godefroy driving, had Cousin Annie and all
my brothers and sisters.

Then Big Sophronie appeared on the threshold carrying me in her
arms. She hoisted herself up on to the leather-backed seat and off we
went to a great thudding of hooves and a crunching of wheels on the
gravel. The other carriages came on after us in a cloud of dust.
All the dogs of the household ran alongside barking their heads
off.

Mother could hear it all up in her bedroom, and she followed the
line of carriages in her thoughts. In two hours' time they would
bring her back her son regenerated by the sacrament of baptism.

Already I had a past behind me—a past of only a few hours'
duration but still a past. There I lay in Sophronie's lap with Tiger
and Jess pulling the big Berlin and Sambo driving. Waiting for me at
the other end of the first journey of my life was the Abbé Dorval
wearing his surplice and standing between two lighted tapers ready to
christen me. What was really waiting for me, what I was really on my
way to meet, was my life.

My life was just beginning; it had indeed already begun.

Out in the country we used to feel the first breath of autumn early.

A few leaves fell from the trees, leaving them a little more denuded each day. The light took on a pellucid quality. Sometimes the atmosphere was charged with moisture and a fine drizzle took the place of the summer thunder-storms. Soon the garden walks were covered with leaves and they lay scattered all over the lawn. Before they shed their last foliage, the trees turned yellow and gold and some went a flaming red. Soon the wind and the rain stripped them of this finery, strewing it over the ground.

Old Sambo raked the leaves together and heaped them up at the bottom of the garden where he set fire to them. Then the smell of burning leaves was wafted into the house. At night, if I woke up, my room seemed full of this pungent odour. There was another fragrance in all the rooms at this time of the year: the smell of burning logs. My mother felt the cold a good deal, so as soon as September came huge fires were lit in the drawing-room and the dining-room.

Fine mists began to steal up from the river and hung suspended above the fields. I had to dress more warmly now before I was let out in the morning to play in the garden.

There were all sorts of things I liked to do there. With the old Negro keeping an eye on me, I would dash up and down the lawn with my dog, or go and look at the burning leaves, or climb up on the wooden fence at the end of the garden and watch the farmer and his son working in the fields beyond. Old Simard ploughed a beautifully straight furrow and it was a pleasure to watch him. I liked to see the ploughshare bite into the earth and throw it up on either side in two thick, brown waves. But my pleasure was all the keener when I could catch a glimpse of my friend Jacques, the eldest of the Simard boys. He was a big, fair lad who seemed very fond of me. I was absolutely devoted to him and loved to watch him driving the team.

Sometimes it was still fairly warm in the afternoons, and then summer seemed to come back for a few hours. My mother used to come out into the garden in a light dress with a scarf around her shoulders. Four o'clock was the time for visitors to arrive, but now tea was served in the drawing-room and not out under the wooden sun-shade, which stuck up from the lawn like a big, green mushroom. Visitors' carriages were driven into the yard behind the house, between the kitchen and the woodshed. You could hear the horses munching and champing, for Godefroy observed the laws of hospitality and brought them out hay and buckets of water.

Ladies' fashions in the nineties were delightful. They wore their hair close to their heads in tight little ringlets, with funny little hats perched up on top. Their skirts had flounces and they sewed rows of buttons on to their bodices, which came to a point at the shoulder. Jet bead trimming glittered richly like a cuirass above swelling bosoms, or was worn in aigrettes on their hats. When I went into the drawing-room to be kissed by all these ladies and to get a big piece of chocolate cake as a reward, this jet gleamed darkly from a whole row of bodices in the half-circle about the fireplace. It was my mother and her "callers" having tea.

Old Sambo acted as butler. Every now and then the reflection of his shiny black face, framed by his white hair, flashed across the mirror. His pink-palmed hands darted about among the guests at shoulder height as he set out china cups and saucers on the table or passed the cream-jug and the sugar-bowl.

Guests generally left about six, and my mother would see them as far as the front steps. That was the place for formal good-byes, while they waited under the porch for their carriages to be led up one behind the other by their coachmen. And so the jet-spangled ladies with their aigrettes winking and nodding in their little hats disappeared into the depths of their black carriages. They drove off to L'Assomption, St. Sulpice, Repentigny, to their moustachioed and side-whiskered husbands, their veranda-girt homes and their drawing-rooms filled with mahogany chairs and dressers. The carriages swung round into the main drive and filed out between the two pillars, each topped by a green ball, before turning into the main highway, which ran along the river. A faint fragrance hung for a few hours in the drawing-room—a fragrance compounded of Florida Water, tea grown cold in the bottoms of cups, and chocolate cake. I saw these "callers" come and go so often that I assumed this happened every day, but I've since found out from my sisters that this social event took place only once a week.

The two Faribault ladies used to call, together with Madame de Martigny, Madame Chaput, Mademoiselle Le Prohon de Beaufort, and others too whose names must be slowly weathering away on the tombstones of village cemeteries. One of the Faribault ladies had a Christian name I liked very much; she was called Laetitia. Madame Chaput's first name was Annie. I never did know what the other visitors were called.

From time to time a very old lady and her daughter came to tea at the manor-house. When my mother knew they were coming, she would send her own carriage to fetch them, because they were too poor to afford a horse and a coachman. These two ladies lived in a small house in L'Assomption Village. They were always treated with marked deference, and when they came into the drawing-room the other ladies lowered their voices. People spoke to them as one speaks to persons who have been especially singled out to be the victims of a great misfortune. Yet this misfortune had occurred a full half-century earlier; in fact, in 1838. These two ladies were Madame and Mademoiselle de Lorimier. The shadow of Montreal Jail hung over the wife and daughter of the Chevalier de Lorimier, the dead "Patriot." Many, many times my mother told me the story of the farewell scene between the condemned man and his wife and daughter.

These two ladies always wore deep mourning; black dresses and black veils. Whenever they came to tea at the manor-house, my mother would ask my sisters and my aunts to look after Mademoiselle de Lorimier. My two aunts were fifteen and eighteen at the time while the Patriot's daughter was nearly sixty. Nevertheless she was still extraordinarily young-looking, with a fresh complexion that reminded one of fruit preserved in syrup. She had the outlook and ideas of a young girl brought up in a small country town.

Madame de Lorimier died in her house at L'Assomption at a great age. Her funeral was made the occasion for a patriotic manifestation of sorts at which the grim events of the Rebellion of 1837 were recalled. Father Dorval seemed greatly moved as he sang the requiem mass for this woman who, for fifty years, had mourned a young husband who met his death on the scaffold. Tributes were paid to Henriette Cadieux de Courville for her misfortune and for her fidelity, but the heroine of the Rebellion carried with her to the grave the secret of her tears, her love, and her long years of sorrow.

Her daughter died a few years later. By that time she had become an invalid and could not leave the house. My Aunt Salaberry told me that she once went to call on her with her mother. They all sat around a little table and drank tea and ate chocolate cake. The Faribault ladies were there as well and Mademoiselle Le Prohon and Madame Chaput.

Towards the end of November, gales would blow up, and the trees would be stripped of all their leaves. A few snowflakes would drift across the expanse of the garden. Indoors, the burnished dogs no longer gleamed in the light from the open fire. Big stoves had to be brought in and set up in the drawing-room and the dining-room. A complicated system of stove-pipes was run along just below the ceiling, and it usually took Godefroy a whole day to install it. The doors of all the rooms were propped open so that the warm air could circulate freely. Godefroy had to put up the double windows too. Then winter could come; the house and the people in it were fully prepared.

At this time of year, an air of foreboding hung over the whole countryside. The big trees along the highway creaked and groaned in the wind as their bare branches were tossed about. The river ran leaden-coloured under grey, deadened skies furrowed by flights of birds in full cry. Every now and then a shot rang out. A hunter, lying in wait in the reeds, had found his mark.

My father used to go hunting with the Simards. Jacques was always the best shot of the whole party.

After these hunting trips, the kitchen table would lie covered with wild duck and partridge. Sophronie the cook and Sophronie the housemaid, with Sambo the Negro to help them, would be hard at work plucking all these birds. Sometimes I used to go in and watch them. The birds' bluish skin struck me as horrible and the drops of dried blood on their beaks used to make me feel quite sick. I felt angry with Jacques for having killed them, but one day, when I told him about it, he burst out laughing. "If you're going to eat them, I've got to kill them first," he said. I was impressed by the logic of his answer. I knew only too well how pleased I was when a dish of partridge cooked with cabbage appeared on the table for dinner. When that happened, the little heads arranged in a circle around the dish didn't bother me in the least. So Jacques taught me that sentimentality can turn into a sort of hypocrisy, for I was well aware that I stood to gain from the crime committed by the hunters.

The snow always came quite suddenly. It would cover the lawn and hide all traces of the walks. It would pile up into white, conical caps on the balls which topped the fence-posts, weighing down the leafless branches, and turning each tree into a glittering bouquet. The white road would soon be streaked with parallel black lines traced out by the wheels of the carts and carriages that drove by our house on the way to Montreal or L'Assomption, but, by the next day, sleighs would have taken their place and the highway would have a hard, icy surface. Against the background of the snow, horse-droppings stood out here and there in high relief—yellow against white.

Sometimes my father or Jacques took me along to the village. When it was Jacques, he would let me hold the reins. The sleigh slid along on the hard, packed snow of the road. As soon as we got to the first houses of the village, Jacques would take over again. There was usually a stop at the blacksmith's or at the general store. Jacques had business to discuss with all sorts of important people. The stop at Archambault's general store was usually a long one. Jacques would go and sit down at the back next to the stove. There was sure to be some crony of his there, so he would pick out one of the wooden arm-chairs for himself and light up his pipe. I would climb up on his lap and usually fall asleep, lulled by the murmur of talk and the heat of the stove.

The big blizzards and the really cold weather usually held off until January or February. December could be quite mild. The snow was "sticky" then and we could build forts with it in the front yard. Jacques once made a snowman by the fence who looked like a sentinel guarding the manor-house. Upside down on his head, he had a saucepan that resembled a uniform cap, and he carried an old broom instead of a rifle.

A little before Christmas, my parents used to make a four-day trip to Montreal. The idea was to buy presents and candy for the holidays. They used to take advantage of their stay to visit relatives and old acquaintances. When they were away, my brothers and sisters and Jacques were given the job of looking after me.

We all spent our evenings together in the kitchen where old Sophronie told us stories.

When my father and mother went off to Montreal, it was a real holiday for us children and for the servants too. Not that my parents were ever tyrannical or fussy; as a matter of fact, they were kindness and understanding personified. But they did insist on certain rules and regulations, and it was fun sometimes to be free of them. For instance, while they were away, we always had supper in the kitchen. There were all sorts of agreeable features about this. The two Sophronies and Godefroy and Sambo the Negro always gave us a hearty welcome to their domain, and Jacques used to be asked in to share the meal with us.

I always made a point of sitting next to him.

The meals Old Sophronie cooked for us were in the best tradition of French-Canadian cuisine: succulent and plentiful. She'd serve us pea soup and pig's trotter stew and pies and pancakes and layer-cakes in profusion. All these good things to eat came straight from the farm, the poultry-run, and the back garden. Food wasn't something that you paid for with money; our whole household fed off the land.

At the manor-house, meals were exactly the same whether they were served in the kitchen or the dining-room. The food Sophronie prepared so skilfully was meant for everybody, and my parents would never have entertained the fantastic notion of eating better than their servants. In fact the very idea would have struck them as downright wicked.

As soon as supper was over, and Sophronie, with the help of Little Sophronie and Sambo, had washed the dishes and tidied up the kitchen, we all took our places again around the big table and Sophronie told us stories.

I can't remember now what they were all about. They were just old stories from the French provinces, part of the romantic folklore of the Mother Country handed down from mother to daughter for generations. Transplanting to America had changed them somewhat and they had acquired a colonial flavour. Old Sophronie, who was a born story-teller, added bits of her own, all sorts of exciting or comic episodes, so that one could listen to the same story twenty times over and it would never be quite the same.

Though I shall probably never be able to recall these stories passed down by oral tradition, I can well remember the evenings spent in the old kitchen, the circle of eager faces, and the sound of the story-teller's voice. It was all full of dramatic lighting and shading, and sometimes I would just sit back and listen to the lilt of it without paying any attention to the story itself. Out beyond the circle where my brothers and sisters sat with Sambo and Jacques, I could see the darkness of the night through the window-panes.

And my imagination peopled the mystery of the night outdoors with the characters the old woman brought to life in her sing-song voice.

When winter really came it changed the whole pattern of our existence in the country to an amazing extent. All the old familiar natural colours and shapes around the house vanished away. The snow and ice turned each landmark into something completely different. The trees were transformed into glittering, aerial creations, set pieces from some display, or destined for the setting of a stage: crystal

B

candelabra, giant bouquets of frosted flowers. Sunshine and shadow played among the ice-sheathed branches creating wonderful, mirror-like effects. Sometimes the falling snow-flakes were great star-like crystals, and the window-panes were frosted over with a tracery of delicate landscapes, which faded slowly away when the sun shone on them.

The whole countryside became a white expanse of desert, and looked empty and inaccessible. Even the garden was now quite different; it had all been changed about. Familiar landmarks were blotted out by the snow and seemed to have disappeared completely. Delicate new patterns, the tracks of birds or of cats, appeared out of nowhere on the surface of the snow that covered the lawn.

Winter cut the manor-house off still more than usual from the outside world. The village now seemed to be very much further away, and we lived in a new silence and a new solitude.

Even people and animals looked different. The horses trotting along the road now pulled light sleighs instead of carriages. A snow-storm changed every horse into a fabulous monster coated with hoar-frost and heralded by the silvery music of the sleigh-bells.

Those sleigh-bells jingling along the white roads of Canada turned every sleigh and sledge into something gay and charming. When an habitant drove by in his *berlot* on the road in front of the house, the sleigh-bells rang out clearly in the cold air. We could hear them from where we sat, snug and warm in the depths of the house. This delicate jingling roused us from our thoughts for a moment and we looked up and listened to the bells as the sound swelled and then died away gently and gradually in the distance. This faint, insistent music of the sleigh-bells was the accompaniment to winter in those days.

My mind and senses were prepared for all these changes when the snow came, and yet this annual miracle never failed to thrill me.

Sometimes it happened overnight, and that would heighten the magic of the effect. When I woke up next morning my room seemed full of light. There were white arabesques dancing on the walls and the ceiling, and I could see from the mirror over the mantelpiece, which always reflected a corner of the garden, that the lawn was covered with snow.

I would jump out of bed and rush to the window, pulling aside the curtains. There was winter, there, just outside.

Part Two

❋

OUT OF THE PAST

As my father and mother were cousins, they shared many of the same ancestors. They were both very much interested in tradition and the past, so the notion of family was always, to our way of thinking, something real and living. My parents would often talk about people who had been dead for fifty or a hundred years, but they spoke of them somehow as if they were still alive. Thus, my father would remark that Charles had suffered a good deal from the gunshot wound he got when he went hunting or that René-Ovide hadn't been particularly happy with his second wife, and I knew he was talking about his great-grandfather and one of his grand-uncles. These old ancestors kept coming in and out of our lives, and in the end they became quite familiar figures. My father's habit of referring to them by their Christian names never bothered me, because I had learned to find my way about among the Charleses, the Renés, the Michels, and the Louis. Some of them were Roquebrunes and others Hertels or Salaberrys.

My father and mother actually lived in the past and looked back to it with real nostalgia. This attitude of theirs raised certain barriers around our own lives. For a long time I really thought that the age into which I had been born was quite unworthy of any interest. Only the past possessed colour and beauty. The present seemed to me an age in which no one ever had adventures any more. The past appeared suffused with an strage charm, but the human race today had lost its joy of living and its sense of beauty. Some dreadful spell had deprived mankind of the spirit of daring. I had been born into a world where nothing ever happened and the whole idea appalled me. My imagination was entirely focused on an age when life was keen, prescient, full of strange adventures, of passionate loves, and peopled with men and women who were likable, attractively odd, and utterly charming.

All families have a past of their own, but most people know nothing about their ancestors. The lives of these men and women are shrouded in complete forgetfulness. Grandchildren know nothing of their grandparents. They have perhaps inherited the features of one of these forgotten forbears, the character of another. Elements which were present in the dead are reassembled in a boy now living or go to make up the loveliness of a young girl's face and features, but death and neglect have wiped out the intervening links.

In our family the past had remained a living reality. My father knew a great deal about it and about our family history, and the topic was a favourite one with him. I think my brothers and sisters used to get rather bored, but I loved it. I thrilled to those dramatic tales of adventure. Of course, there are families where nothing ever happens for centuries. These are very dull ones. Ours, on the other hand, was an amusing one, because it had been full of people who lived like heroes straight out of a novel or a play.

My father's family name was La Roque de Roquebrune; my mother's Irumberry de Salaberry. The Roquebrunes came from Gascony and were an army family. The Salaberrys were Basques and were a seafaring lot. In Louis XIV's day, there was a regiment called the Régiment de La Roque. The colonel was one of our ancestors, La Roque de Saint-Chamarand. Under Louis XV, the four admirals, who were known as the Admirals of the Eastern and Western Oceans, were respectively La Rochefoucauld d'Amville, Broglie, Court de La Bruère, and Salaberry de Benneville. "It's thanks to his cousin La Roque de Saint-Chamarand," my father used to say, "that our first Canadian ancestor managed to wriggle out of the scrape he had got into by fighting a duel with Hauterive. And it was his cousin the admiral who gave the first Canadian Salaberry a leg-up in his naval career. It was a good thing to have relatives in those days.

"French aristocrats in the past used to use several family names. Some of them were taken from properties they owned or were surnames that came to them through their wives. They followed the same fashion when they emigrated to Canada. The Joyberts were also called Marsan and Soulanges, the Rigauds Vaudreuil and Cavagnal, while the Bouchers used names like Boucherville, Montizambert, Niverville, La Broquerie, La Perrière, and Grandpré. People nowadays sometimes think that it was for snobbish reasons that the French used so many names, but anybody who thinks that simply doesn't understand how things were done in those days. It was because they were individualists that members of a same family used different names. The family itself could always be distinguished by a surname that didn't vary, but each member added other family names to his own."

This practice survived into the nineteenth century. My father called himself Hertel, which was his mother's maiden name. The Hertels are of Norman descent and have played a distinguished part in Canadian history through François de Hertel and his son Hertel de Rouville. The former, under Count Frontenac, carried the war into New England in 1690. The latter fought over the same territory in 1708, under the Marquis de Vaudreuil. The American historian Parkman has told the tale of this fierce frontier war and of its battles and calls the Hertels "bloodthirsty ruffians," but the Abbé de Charlevoix in his *History* says that they were "the heroes of New France."

For me, the history of Canada was a story told in the evenings, under the lamp-light—almost a fairy-story. And it was my father's words that gave shape and substance to this illustrious past.

As I listened to him, the phrases he uttered turned into the men and women of days gone by. Their faces came to life, their deeds, their loves, the dangers they ran, and their tragic deaths.

"All families are old families," he used to say. "The Durands and the Martins go back just as far as the Montmorencys or the Rohans. It would be really interesting to know the story of the Durands and be possible to write them up. Michelet wanted to be the historian of the French people, but he never managed it, because historians inevitably concentrate on the history of great men and never on that of the people. What you find in Michelet is Joan of Arc and Robespierre, not the men and women of the Hundred Years' War or the French Revolution."

My father had very original ideas about history and it was a subject that always brought him out of himself. He had read so many old documents! These family trees and officers' commissions and private letters filled three huge green folders, and, together with his own recollections and the traditional lore that had come down to him from his parents, they comprised the history of the family. "These La Roques and Roquebrunes weren't really particularly important people," he used to say. "They were just good soldiers like all Gascons. They weren't rich either, and the seigneuries of La Roque and of Roquebrune for which Bernard de La Roque paid homage and swore fealty to the Count of Armagnac in 1409 were really just small farms, which they often tilled with their own hands. Gascons were poverty-stricken but proud. They called themselves counts and barons, bore a whole host of names, and proved their noble descent on parchments registered with the Provincial Intendant, but their clothes were often in rags and they were glad to marry off their daughters to peasant farmers while their sons served the King in regiments that were the private property of illustrious kinsmen of theirs. Under the Old Régime, regiments actually belonged to their colonels. The Régiment de La Roque, which was owned by La Roque de Saint-Chamarand, had been bought from the King for cash. For the King of France was in trade like any other big business man. Offices that carried the privilege of nobility, regiments, jobs as collectors of taxes, all formed part of the royal stock-in-trade. As the La Roque de Saint-Chamarands were wealthy, they could afford to buy a regiment for their eldest son. This money came down to them from the Peyronnencs. Philibert de Roquebrune served as a lieutenant in his cousin's regiment. His mother was a Mercilly and his grandmother a Couillaud-Hauteclair. Being a Marcilly or a Couillaud doesn't count for anything nowadays, but in the seventeenth century they were influential people in the provinces of Orléans and Angoulême. La Roque used Couillaud, his grandmother's family name, as a surname. It gave him a link with the magistracy, for the Couillaud de Hauteclairs had been judges. This young lieutenant was an ambitious fellow and meant to get on in the world by using all these relations. But he went and fought this duel with Hauterive and that changed the whole story."

My father usually puffed away at a pipe as he talked. In my memory, these old family tales are somehow fragrant with the odour of the Canadian tobacco he smoked in his stubby clay pipe. The past seemed to float for an instant beneath the rafters before evaporating in a bluish haze. I could just make out vague shapes and faces, which appeared only to disappear again. When he was at a loss for a name or a date he would often go and fetch one of the green cardboard folders from the dusk in the drawing-room. Then he would open it out on the table and take out letters and commissions and appointments. And he would put his finger under the royal signature, the elegant, ornate "Louis," and say, "You see, you see, it's signed by the King."

"Nobody has ever found out who this Hauterive was or why Roquebrune fought a duel with him, but the silliest thing a young officer could do in Louis XIV's time was to get mixed up in a duel, for the laws against duelling were severe. If one of the contestants died, the survivor was tried for murder and ran the risk of having his head cut off. Roquebrune was shielded by La Roque de Saint-Chamarand.

"At that time the young man had left the Régiment de La Roque and had joined the Black Musketeers. As the Musketeers formed part of the Household Troops, anyone who wanted to get in to the regiment had to prove his noble birth. Roquebrune passed the test. Because of their democratic notions, many people find these old rules absurd, but they were quite consistent really, and there was a good reason for them. In those days, nobody had to serve in the wars unless they were of noble birth or liked fighting. Soldiering was a trade like any other. Neither the townspeople nor the merchants nor the peasants were forced by the King to take arms. Soldiers were volunteers. As for the nobles, it was their bounden duty to fight, for if they were exempt from paying their taxes in money, it was only right that they should make up for it by paying them in blood."

At this point my father would break off his story to go and fetch the family tree from the drawer in the desk. It was spread over four pages turned yellow with age and even the ink had rusted. "None of this really amounts to much," he would say. "The Roquebrunes don't really go back very far and they weren't a particularly illustrious family. Before this Bernard de La Roque and his vow of homage and fealty in 1409 there is really nothing. They seem to have been very proud of a marriage contracted in the sixteenth century with a member of the Esparbès family and of another marriage with this Couillaud whose name they persisted in using for two or three generations. There was a Ferrabouc bride too; their arms were 'a ram passant on a field argent.' But who were the Ferraboucs? Coats-of-arms were really puzzles of a kind and served to designate families just as their surnames did. As for the Roquebrunes, their coat-of-arms, charged with a cross saltire and a rock mortised sable, quartered with three stars, showed from the quartering that they were a younger branch. All these rules were clearly understood at the time, the heraldic objects, called 'charges,' were just a sort of shorthand. Three hundred years from now, our great-grandnephews won't understand our own age any better than we understand the periods in which our ancestors lived, and our customs, our pecularities, our ways of life will seem as odd to them as those of the men and women of the seventeenth century appear to us.

"When his career as a Musketeer had been ruined by this silly duel, Roquebrune was presented by La Roque de Saint-Chamarand to the Marquis de Chastelard-Sallières and got a commission in the Régiment de Carignan-Sallières. The Prince de Carignan had been colonel of this regiment and they had retained his name. Philibert de Roquebrune was posted to Contrecœur's company, fought in the campaign against the Turks, and, in 1665, took ship at La Rochelle and sailed with his regiment for Canada. After fighting the Turks, Carignan-Sallières was sent to do battle against the Iroquois. The Viceroy of New France in those days was the Marquis de Tracy. He was a seasoned campaigner hailing from Picardy. He knew a lot about strategy and fought brilliantly against the Iroquois. When they had been beaten by the men of Carignan-Sallières, the Indians made peace, and it was then that the King made his bid to induce the officers and men of the regiment to stay on in the colony.

"All the younger ones accepted. Roquebrune was thirty. As the younger son of a younger son, the only future he could look forward to in France was being posted from one garrison town to another and ending his days as a captain on half pay. His father Bernard de La Roque was dead. The Château de La Roque in Gascony and the Roquebrune estates belonged to the elder branch. The only thing he had, to use the expression current in those days, was an honourable name. Most of the officers and men of the Carignan regiment were in the same boat. Saint-Ours, Contrecœur, Sorel, Verchères, Gautier de Varennes all decided to stay on. Saint-Ours had a château in Dauphiné, but it was in ruins. Varennes had lands in Anjou, but they were mortgaged to the hilt. Contrecœur had been ruined by a lawsuit. All these soldiers had better prospects in Canada than back home in France; so they stayed. Acting in the King's name, the Governor gave them seigneuries along the St. Lawrence, on the Island of Montreal, or up the Richelieu. Seigneuries! The word sounds impressive, so much more impressive than what it actually stood for. After working for twenty years on his seigneurie, Eschaillon de Saint-Ours still had to do his own ploughing with the help of his sons and daughters."

My father dug down into one of the green cardboard folders and retrieved a sheet of paper. "The seal of Notary Basset! In 1667, Canada was still quite wild and there weren't many more than ten thousand Frenchmen in the whole colony. Montreal was a little wooden town with a palisade around it. The habitants' houses were fortified and when they tilled their fields they kept their muskets fastened to their ploughs. The Massacre of 1690 is a good enough indication of what the colonists were up against, and yet there were notaries in every centre of population. This document, signed by Notary Bénigne Basset, and dated from Montreal on September 24, 1667, states that 'Roquebrune of Contrecœur's company' owns one acre of land on the Island of Montreal in the Urbain Boudreau concession. The officers and the men of the Carignan regiment were settlers now. Every French-Canadian family today can trace its descent from at least one of the soldiers of that glorious regiment.

"They married local girls, the daughters of the men who had accompanied Monsieur de Maisonneuve when he founded Montreal. And, as there weren't enough wives for all these soldiers, the King sent out others by the shipload. They were brought out to Quebec under the supervision of one of the ladies of the colony, Madame Bourdon; others were chaperoned by nuns. They were officers' daughters and the King gave each one a dowry. Bachelor settlers flocked to Quebec and the Governor held informal receptions at the Château Saint-Louis to enable the young people to get to know one another. A fortnight after one of these shiploads of brides had arrived, they would all be married off. The young couples were ready to set off from Quebec harbour in their birchbark canoes, bound for a clearing 'below Quebec' or in the vicinity of Three Rivers or Montreal. The knots had all been tied by the Bishop himself. These frail canoes, bobbing on the waters of the great river, cradled many a French-Canadian family of the future.

"Philibert de Roquebrune didn't have to go to Quebec for a wife because he found one ready to hand in Montreal in the home of one of the habitants, Jacques de La Porte de Saint-Georges, who had a grant at St. Marie and was one of the richest settlers on the island. Back in Berry, the Saint-Georges estates had belonged to the La Portes ever since the fifteenth century. Yet Jacques de La Porte had

left Berry and its tranquillity to become an habitant on the Island of
Montreal. It was a curious business. The big island with its mountain
rising out of the expanse of the broad river bore no resemblance to
the landscape of Berry. These French founders of the colony were
many of them escapists with a gnawing, secret hunger for a change
of scene. Canada had a special fascination for men of a certain type.
The propaganda put out by the Jesuits, and by the pious Madame de
Bullion, found its way into the homes of many devout men and
women. Whole families went off to Canada with the sole purpose of
living as the early Christians had done before them. It seemed easier
to lead a pious life overseas, and Heaven then was not so far away.
Chomedey de Maisonneuve, Lambert Closse, Marguerite Bourgeoys,
Madame d'Ailleboust, and many of the other first settlers of Montreal were mystics lit by an inner flame. La Porte de Saint-Georges
left France for Canada to save his soul.

"He had had sons and daughters. They all lived in a fortified house
at St. Marie, which was out in the country beyond the walls of
Montreal. La Roque de Roquebrune lived in a fortified house too, at
St. Martin, near the river. The young officer turned settler had for
his nearest neighbours two habitants, Elie Baujon and Jacques Brias,
nicknamed 'Soldier' Brias. They probably gave each other a hand
when the Indians were on the war-path, and that happened often
enough. A cannon fired from the fort at Montreal was the usual
signal that Indians had been sighted on the Island. Everybody rushed
home from the fields as fast as possible. Doors were closed and barred
and all loopholes manned. But there weren't alarms of this sort all
the time. There were only certain critical periods when the Iroquois
were particularly threatening. The year 1690 was the worst year of
all. In normal times Montreal had a miniature social life all its own.
After all, Frenchmen are sociable by nature. Put a group of French
people down anywhere and they will set up a human pattern of existence for themselves. These traits are predetermined by race and by
a deep-set, civilizing urge. Canada had its own 'society' right from
the beginnings of things. The Island of Montreal with its little walled-
in area, its palisaded farm-houses, its fields, its gardens, and its
orchards constituted a social world—a social world in microcosm,
but possessed of plenty of courage and graciousness, though ruled by
a rather formal politeness and by military discipline. The Governor
of the Island, whoever he might be—Monsieur Boisberthelot de
Beaucours, the Chevalier de Callières, or Monsieur Le Moyne de

Longueuil—gave a round of receptions and dinners. High Mass at
the parish church on Sundays was quite an event. The Sulpician
Order provided all the parish clergy and these Sulpicians were of
gentle birth and knew how to behave in polite society. The Superior
of the Order, Monsieur Dollier de Casson, had been an officer in
Marshal Turenne's army before taking orders. The Governor
General of the colony—Count Frontenac or the Marquis de Denon-
ville—used to come up from Quebec once a year to spend a few
weeks in Montreal. That was the real social season. Everyone went
to the balls the Governor gave, and on Sundays the Sulpician Church
was crammed to the doors because everybody wanted to see His
Excellency seated before his *prie-dieu* in the choir. The Récollet
Church was quite fashionable too, mainly because of the magnificent
sermons on sin preached by Father Olivier Goyer. As a matter of
fact, there were scandals and illicit love-affairs then that caused a
good deal of gossip. The Chevalier de Callières and Madame de
Ramezay were a favourite topic. Mademoiselle de Belestre took a
paternity suit before the Colonial Council against Pierre d'Iberville.
French Canadians in those days were as inflammable as they were
heroic. Their women knew how to fight but they also knew how to
make love. Madeleine de Verchères defended her family's fort against
the Iroquois with the aid of one soldier and her two small brothers.
Madame de Drucour fired the cannon of Louisbourg against the
English with her own hand, but Angélique Desmeloizes, Marguerite
de Martigny, Madame de Beaubassin were the respective mistresses
of the Intendant Bigot, of the Chevalier de Lévis, and of the Marquis
de Montcalm. Canadians were hot-blooded in those days."

My father seemed preoccupied by a train of thought and sucked
for a while at his pipe. "Roquebrune spent a good deal of his time at
the Saint-Georges'. In winter he would put on his snow-shoes and
race across the snow to St. Marie. Then he would spend the evening
by the fireside with his friends. Monsieur de La Porte would talk
about France and about Berry. Roquebrune would tell about the
campaigns he had fought, about the Battle of Gothard, about his life
as a Musketeer or as an officer in the Régiment de La Roque. With
his own eyes he had seen the King at Versailles. The girls of the
family hung on his lips, for they had been born in Montreal and had
never even seen France. This French officer seemed a terribly important person and quite entranced them. They must have lain awake
at nights thinking about him. Suzanne-Catherine de Saint-Georges

grew particularly fond of him. She used to sit on his knee to hear him tell his stories. There is nothing particularly remarkable about that because she was only thirteen at the time. Madame de La Porte certainly didn't see anything wrong in it. She took it for granted that one day he would ask for the hand of one of her daughters. And that is just what happened; he chose Suzanne.

"She had violet-coloured eyes, long silky hair, and a rather large mouth. In her long grey homespun dress with its white collar she already looked quite a grown-up little person and she was lively and charming. This little Montreal blossom quite bewitched the ex-soldier. He had spent all his life in barracks and camps, in the company of rough men, of horses and of weapons, and he fell head over heels in love with her. There wasn't anything unusual about this in Canada, where, by the King's command, girls married at fifteen and young men at eighteen.

"La Roque de Roquebrune wanted Monseigneur de Montmorency-Laval to perform the ceremony. He had a special veneration for the Bishop of the Colony, who was indeed a saintly figure. So they all set off by canoe from the foot of the rapids. Monsieur and Madame de Saint-Georges travelled with their children in one craft and in the other was Roquebrune with Elie Baujon and Jacques 'Soldier' Brias. In this way they set out for Quebec. People had to use the river route, as in those days no road had yet been cut through the forest. The great canoes danced up and down over the waves. The trip down to Quebec didn't actually take long: a matter of four or five days. The travellers took their food and muskets along with them. Once in the capital, there was usually a reception at the Château Saint-Louis where the Governor kept open house. The marriage of the officer and the young girl was blessed by Monseigneur de Montmorency. The Bishop was an old man, tall and bald-headed, worn to a shadow by his austerities. The sacred ornaments he wore had been given by Anne of Austria or by the Duchess d'Aiguillon, the great patron of the missions to Canada. The journey back to Montreal was a slow business, for paddling against the current was hard work. At sunset they went ashore to spend the night in a tent on the beach. One man kept watch, walking up and down with his dog who would growl at the slightest sound, even if it was only the wind blowing through the grass, rustling a leaf, stirring a branch.

One evening they came in sight of Montreal just at moonrise. In the distance, from the middle of the great island, the outline of the mountain seemed to brood over the quiet waters of the St. Lawrence. Roquebrune had long since dropped his paddle, for his girl-bride had crept into his arms, and he held her cradled against his heart. She was asleep, and he couldn't move for fear of waking her. Elie Baujon in the bow, and in the stern Jacques Brias—"Soldier" Brias—sang softly as they paddled. The other canoe came on behind. The rhythm of the song kept time for the paddles. French Canadians always sang on the water; it made the work easier. When they stepped ashore below the fort at Montreal, the girl was still asleep, and Roquebrune still bore his slender burden. He cut across the fields by paths he knew well as he had followed them so often, and so came home with his wife asleep against his shoulder."

I always liked that story. It gave me an odd feeling of delight. What pleased me most about the romance of my ancestor and his young wife was its tenderness. When my father paused at the end, it was as if we had arrived at the threshold of that house in the fields outside Montreal—the threshold our first Canadian ancestor crossed on his wedding-night with a young girl asleep in his arms. That was really the end of the story. "What more do you want me to tell you? They lived happily ever after. Anybody could be happy in Canada in those days. There was plenty of everything. Nobody had even heard of money; there was scarcely a single coin in circulation in the whole colony. But that didn't last long; Montreal's Golden Age was drawing to a close. The French Canadians started to trade with the Indians for furs. Louis de Roquebrune took a hand in that; he was the son of the officer and of Suzanne de Saint-Georges. He married a Sabourin and with his cousin, the Chevalier de Tonty, who had also married a Sabourin, he set off for the *pays d'en haut*. Tonty, who was also called Tonty Desliettes, which was his grandmother's surname, was the son of the commander of Fort Pontchartrain, built on one of the Great Lakes. He was also the nephew of the famous Tonty Bras-de-Fer. They were an adventurous family, comrades-in-arms of Cavalier de La Salle and great builders of forts. Roquebrune set out with Tonty by canoe, went down the Mississippi as far as Louisiana, and it was two years before he came back to his wife who lived on a seigneurie near the Lake of Two Mountains. There stood his manor-house and it was there that he died at a great age, leaving a fortune to his son."

My father put down his pipe and drew an officer's commission out of one of the green folders. "This is a lieutenant's commission in the Régiment de Berry made out to Louis La Roque de Roquebrune. Lots of men were called Louis then because of the King. This was the son of the man who had paddled up and down the rivers of America with Tonty. This document is dated 1759 and is signed by the colonel, Monsieur de Trivio. On September 13, 1759, Roquebrune fought on the Plains of Abraham along with his comrades in the Régiments de Berry, de Guyenne, de La Sarre, de Languedoc, and de La Colonie, all under the command of the Marquis de Montcalm. You know the upshot of that battle outside Quebec. Montcalm was killed, the French army was defeated after a heroic struggle and the capital of Canada fell to the British. On the British side, the Highland regiment commanded by Lord Lovat played what was probably a decisive part in the battle. An entire company of McDonalds were in the line opposite Berry. Roquebrune, who was a good shot like most French Canadians, brought down more than one of them, but memories of this occasion didn't prevent his son from marrying, in 1781, the daughter of Captain Daniel McDonald. And I knew the Scotswoman's son, for he was my grandfather and lived till 1859.

"He was christened Charles after Charles Stuart, because his mother, Geneviève McDonald, was a fervent Jacobite. People in that day and age were capable of remaining faithful for years on end to a sovereign or a personal hero. Because of his veneration for Louis XVI, the Martyr King, and for General Sir Isaac Brock, the hero of the War of 1812, my grandfather called his son Louis-Isaac.

"In any stock, the human type can change all of a sudden, the mother's ancestral characteristics replacing those of the father. Then, with the second generation, atavism comes into play again, and there is a reversion to paternal traits and cast of countenance. That's what happened in the case of our family. Charles de Roquebrune was six feet tall and had fair hair. He was a real Scotsman and looked like the McDonalds, but his son Louis was dark and of medium height. He had blue-black hair—a regular Gascon."

I heard all this talk in snatches. My father used to come back to the subject every now and then, adding a touch here and there, or filling in with additional detail. It had all been handed on to him by his grandfather, so the chronicle came to me by word of mouth and from a long way off, as if each generation in turn were telling me its own story.

"Charles and Louis were complete opposites in their ideas too.

The father was a Royalist, who thought Louis XVI a saint, liked the British, and admired Sir Isaac Brock, but Louis had revolutionary notions. He was a devotee of the French Revolution and his hero was Napoleon. This was normally a source of dissension, but in 1837, at the time of the Rebellion, their antagonism turned to tragedy, for they found themselves on opposite sides. Because of his Scottish mother, Charles de Roquebrune spoke English well, and this was a help to him in the business world. He also had many English friends, which was another circumstance that helped to enrich him. The French Canadians had been ruined by the Conquest and by the Seven Years' War. There had never been much hard money in circulation in the colony, and the Royal Intendant had introduced a sort of paper currency called 'card money.' It consisted of bills payable by the Crown. After 1765, the British bought up all this paper money for a song and resold it to Louis XV at face value. Both seigneurs and habitants lost millions over this transaction."

My father sent a puff of bluish smoke up towards the ceiling. After hanging above us for a moment, the smoke thinned out and then vanished. "In the eighteenth century, the French Canadians made money with their beaver pelts and their lumber. All Europe wore beaver hats that had originated in New France. The hulls and the masts of French ships were made of timber from Canada. From 1700 down to the Conquest, we supplied the Paris hatters and all the ship-building yards. The three-cornered hat worn by Marshal Saxe at the Battle of Fontenoy and the mainmast of Comte de la Gallissonnière's flagship at Port Mahon may very well have come from one of our seigneuries. After the Peace of Paris, which handed us over to the British, French Canada was bankrupt. Some families still owned land in the form of seigneuries, but these brought in no income, so many sold out to the British. The Roquebrunes were as impoverished as the rest, but they hung on to their lands. As a consequence, by 1800, Charles hadn't a penny to his name but he was the seigneur of a vast extent of uncleared land in Ontario. His business sense he inherited from the McDonalds, because there is nothing Gascon about that. Like most French Canadians of his day, he was practically illiterate, but he knew how to figure. With a Scotsman for a partner, he built a sawmill on his Ontario properties at a place he called Roqueville. After a few years, he had become a large-scale exporter of lumber to the British market. As he was enterprising and imaginative like all business men, he opened up stores in both Quebec and

Ontario, and built a village around his manor-house at Roqueville with a church where the Abbé Saya officiated. He took his first trip to Britain in 1816. In Scotland he went to call on the McDonalds and visited Lord Coldwell, who was a cousin of his. He went to Paris, too, and saw Louis XVIII. For French Canadians, the Bourbons were still 'the Royal Family.' Out of family piety he also went to Gascony. The elder branch were still living in the Château de La Roque and there he saw 'the Family.' It was represented by an old gentleman who received him with great politeness and told him stories about the Army of the Princes. He also served him an excellent armagnac and gave him the bedroom where Philibert de Roquebrune had slept two hundred years before."

One day my father took me into his bedroom, opened a big cupboard, and took a coat out of one of the drawers. It was made of blue cloth and had a high velvet collar. It was fastened with carved gilt buttons over a shirt with a lace jabot.

"This is the coat Louis de Roquebrune wore in 1840, the day he was married to Henriette Hertel de Rouville. The ushers were Georges Etienne Cartier and Thomas Lewis Drummond. All four of these young people had shared moments of great danger during the Rebellion of 1837. Etienne Cartier and La Roque de Roquebrune fought against the British in the Valley of the Richelieu in the ranks of the Patriot Army. Cartier managed to reach the border but Roquebrune was taken prisoner and spent a year in Montreal Jail in the shadow of General Colborne's gallows. Drummond, who was a lawyer, defended the French-Canadian patriots before the courts martial, and managed to save a good many of them from the hangman's noose. As for Henriette de Rouville, she was a secret agent of the patriots in the Richelieu Valley all through the dramatic autumn of 1837."

He put the blue coat back in the drawer and started pacing up and down the room. I was sitting in an arm-chair with my legs tucked up under me as I listened to him talking about the Rebellion. "In 1837, my father was twenty-five and my mother twenty. He lived at Rigaud in a big white house built by Charles de Roquebrune, while she lived in the manor-house at St. Hilaire, on the Richelieu. They had never met. Louis de Roquebrune quite often went to Montreal, either on horseback or in a *calèche*. He also used to go hunting in Ontario and spent weeks at a time on his property at Roqueville. But he liked

Montreal better. He belonged to the Sons of Liberty and used to listen to the speeches of Papineau and Dr. Chénier. Many French Canadians disliked the British and wanted to get rid of them. Their dream was of a French-Canadian republic, and Cartier and Drummond had all sorts of plans in this connection. Drummond was a young Irishman and hated everything English. It was his belief that Papineau would one day be President of the Republic of Canada. Feelings ran high in the province of Quebec, and there were the beginnings of revolt in Ontario too. The Governor, Lord Gosford, tried to make the French Canadians see reason, but General Colborne was only waiting for a chance to stamp out a movement which spelled danger for a British colony. There was rioting in the streets of Montreal but most of the patriot forces were concentrated in the counties of Two Mountains and Richelieu. Colonel Gore, an old soldier who had fought at Waterloo, attacked the Patriots entrenched round the little village of St. Denis on the Richelieu. The French Canadians kept up a steady fire from the windows of the houses, and the red coats were obliged to retreat, leaving their dead in the village streets and abandoning their guns. Roquebrune, sheltered behind the shutters of a house in St. Denis, blazed away at the British all through that day. Many of the Sons of Liberty were killed. Those who survived were drunk with victory, and Roquebrune was particularly delighted at having helped defeat a former adversary of Napoleon. But the Battle of St. Charles, at the end of November 1837, spelled disaster for the French Canadians. General Wetherall was in command of the British troops there, and he cut the Patriots up badly. Papineau and Cartier managed to escape and take refuge in the United States. The rebels now had a price on their heads. General Colborne posted an offer of four thousand dollars' reward for Papineau, dead or alive; the others were priced at five hundred apiece."

My father at this point was standing in front of the window, looking out into the garden, and seemed to be watching events as he described them. His rather deep voice took on a musical cadence. "Your grandfather was an enterprising young man and had a cool head on his shoulders. He managed to get through the British lines. With two companions, Bonaventure Viger and Lambert, he made of way across country, hiding every now and then behind clumps of bushes. An habitant let them take refuge on his farm. They were covered in dust and their hands were black with powder, so they couldn't have hidden the fact that they were rebels. The three of them together were worth fifteen hundred dollars, which was a small fortune in 1837, but the habitants were all Patriots and Sons of Liberty. They helped the rebels all through the grim months of the insurrection in spite of the excommunications fulminated against them by the Bishop of Montreal, Monseigneur Lartigue, who had got cold feet. The country clergy, on the other hand, blessed the muskets of the rebels and gave them absolution before they went into battle.

"The three rebels crossed the Richelieu and hid at the Drolet place at St. Marc. They had tried to get to the border, but it was a long way off. The news was very bad. Martial law had been proclaimed by the Colonial Governor, and the Patriots were being made to stand their trial before courts martial. A scaffold awaited the condemned in the yard of Montreal Jail.

"After they had had a bit of a rest, the three started off again. At a bend in the road they sighted a body of British troops commanded by an officer on horseback. They were guarding a group of French-Canadian prisoners who had their hands tied behind their backs. The three Sons of Liberty still had their muskets with them, so they hid in a ditch and waited for the British to come within range. 'Pick your man,' said Viger in a matter-of-fact tone of voice. 'I'm taking the one with the white plumes.' 'Good,' said Lambert, 'then I'll take the one with the red ones.' That left Roquebrune to cope with the rank and file.

"They fired, and the British, who were taken by surprise, stopped in their tracks. Every shot found its mark. To get more freedom of action, Viger and Roquebrune put their grey top-hats, called 'beaver hats,' on the side of the ditch, but Lambert kept his on. A return volley came from the British ranks, and Lambert's hat was holed in several places. So he yelled in his rage, 'You've ruined my hat, you damned English; I'll make you pay for it.' And then he started blazing away like a madman. In fact the three men were able to keep up such a rapid and accurate fire that the British thought they had fallen into an ambush, so they withdrew and were soon out of sight. Some of their prisoners had taken advantage of the scuffle to get free, and they joined forces with the three heroes of this remarkable engagement.

"The Patriots weren't quite sure what to do now, so they headed for the village of Belœil. It started to rain. All the houses seemed deserted. The inhabitants were afraid the British were coming and dared not open their doors. Still, information was vital. Was the road clear as far as Chambly? After that it was no great distance to the American border.

"Not far from the Belœil church a rider appeared down the road and came towards them at a gallop. Roquebrune went forward, but when the rider drew a little closer he saw it was a woman. She reined in her horse and the young man looked at her admiringly, because she was distinctly pretty. She returned his glance. Here was one of the heroes of the campaign along the Richelieu. She admired his proud look and his brave courage. Everything about him carried the assurance of courage and confidence. In her eyes, this young man, splashed with mud from head to foot, was the symbol of struggle, of country, and of the purity of sacrifice. Henriette de Rouville was a Patriot too. Ever since the early days of the Rebellion, she had been galloping up and down the countryside keeping the French Canadians posted about the movements of enemy troops. Her father, Hertel de Rouville, like many other seigneurs and members of the higher clergy, was on the government side, and had agreed to let General Wetherall's men bivouac in the grounds of his manor-house at St. Hilaire. Henriette was furious and went off to live with an habitant family in one of the farm-houses. 'Don't go through Belœil,' she warned Roquebrune. 'General Wetherall is encamped in the manor-house grounds at St. Hilaire. There are red coats on both banks of the river. You'll have to circle around through the woods, behind the farms. When you get to Chambly, avoid the town itself; go around it. Colonel Gore's stationed there.' Then the girl on horseback dashed off at full gallop. She turned once in her saddle to point with her riding-crop at a path that led into the woods.

"The three fugitives took the girl's advice and managed to get as far as the border, but they were arrested by the military police before they could set foot on American soil. They put up a fierce fight and stout-hearted Lambert was killed. Viger and Roquebrune, now in despair, were prisoners in the hands of General Colborne. They were taken to Montreal Jail and stayed there many months waiting trial. There were over five hundred Patriots with them, all under threat of death. The rising had collapsed completely. At St. Eustache, in the county of Two Mountains, Dr. Chénier himself had been killed heading the rebels. A court-martial was set up under the presidency of General Sir John Clitherow. Young Drummond, the lawyer, defended those who stood in greatest peril and managed to save some of them from the gallows: there was Prieur, for instance, who was transported to Australia. But Hamelin, Daunais, the two brothers Sanguinet, the Chevalier de Lorimier, Pierre de Coigne, Narbonne, and others were condemned and executed. As they were British subjects, they were accused of bearing arms against Her Majesty's Government. This charge was true. They were also accused of high treason, and this charge was false. They were all young men, for the Rebellion of 1837 was essentially a youthful undertaking. They came from all classes of society. Cardinal, one of those executed, was a notary and just over thirty. Thomas de Lorimier was younger than that. Ambroise Sanguinet, seigneur of La Prairie, was twenty-five. He was hanged along with his brother. François Hamelin, who shared the same fate, was an habitant and only twenty-three. Among all the condemned there was only one man as old as fifty: that was Joseph Robert, a farmer. These men had dreamed of a French-speaking republic on the shores of the St. Lawrence. That was their only crime. They certainly did not deserve to die.

"The last hours of the Chevalier Thomas de Lorimier were agonizing. His young wife came to say good-bye to him in his cell with their little daughter in her arms. The poor woman fainted and had to be carried out. Lorimier was steadfast to the end. The other prisoners were allowed to come and shake hands with him. Just before he set out for the gallows, he asked Prieur to help him adjust his cravat. 'Loosen it,' he said quite calmly. 'Loosen it; it will get in the way of the rope.'

"All Canada was horrified by the ferocity of these repressive measures. Even in England people protested. The British government was very embarrassed, for the American press began publishing hostile articles. So Lord Durham was sent out to conduct his famous inquiry. He favoured a certain indulgence and wanted to pacify the colony. As time went by, death sentences were commuted to transportation, and in the end General Sir John Clitherow fined the remaining rebels heavily and let them go free.

"Charles de Roquebrune had been furious ever since the beginning of the Rebellion. He was furious with his son, furious with the British, furious with Monseigneur Lartigue, furious with Lord Gosford, but of course he wanted to save young Roquebrune. Drummond advised him not to draw attention to the prisoner in his cell and to keep getting the trial postponed. The young lawyer considered that the best thing to do was to play for time. He was quite right; when Roquebrune came up for trial in July 1838, death sentences had rather gone out of fashion and so had transportation to penal settlements. Roquebrune got off with a fine of a thousand pounds, which his father was only too happy to pay.

"The young rebel resumed his former existence as an easy-going, idle young man of fashion. He hunted on the Ontario estates and went to the theatre in Montreal to applaud the French actresses from Louisiana who came up on tour. He went out and about a lot too. After the dramatic years of 1837 and 1838, people felt they had to forget and sought distraction and amusement. The 1840 winter season in Montreal was a particularly brilliant one, with a continuous round of balls and dinner-parties. There was a good deal of entertaining too in the manor-houses out in the country. All the girls and young women adored the rebels. These young fellows who had fought along the Richelieu and beside the Lake of Two Mountains were heroes in their eyes; they had triumphed over death.

"A young man and a young woman suddenly came face to face at a ball given by the Lotbinière-Harwoods at their manor-house at Vaudreuil. They had met once before on a road in the rain in November 1837. Their meeting had lasted only a minute or two, but she had often thought about the young man with the proud face and the steadfast eyes. And he, in his prison, waiting for death, had dreamed of the fine-looking girl on horseback, and it had given him fresh courage to go on hoping."

At this point, my father would stop for a few moments and seem to be casting his mind back. "I do believe," he would say finally, "I do believe they fell in love that very first time. La Roque de Roquebrune and Henriette Hertel de Rouville got married a few months later, but their love was born in that fleeting moment when they first met in the midst of danger and flight and violence."

"Those Hertels on my mother's side of the family were all soldiers," my father often said. "The first one we have any record of was called Thomas de Hertel and he was one of the defenders of the Mont St. Michel under Estouteville during the siege of 1425. His name is on the roll of knights who formed part of the permanent garrison."

My father opened one of the green folders and leafed through the papers. "Fighting was their profession whether in France or in Canada. Jacques Hertel de la Fresnière came out to the colony with a batch of troops dispatched by the Company of the Hundred Associates. Richelieu was minister at the time and he had granted this company development rights in New France. Hertel turned colonist and was given land in the Three Rivers district. When he died, in 1651, he left a huge estate to his son, but it was all covered in dense forest. François de Hertel was brought up by his mother, who had contracted a second marriage with an officer by the name of Moral de Saint-Quentin. She was a Marguerie from Rouen and hence a Norman like the Hertels. This woman was absolutely devoted to her son whom she called Fanchon. The man who was destined to become such a formidable warrior in the border wars was always Fanchon to this great-hearted woman. He himself always used this diminutive to sign the magnificent letters he wrote to Father Le Moyne and which were later published in the Jesuit *Relations* for 1662."

My father showed me the actual volume put out by Cramoizie, who was the Jesuits' Paris publisher. "These *Relations* were made up from the letters sent from Quebec by the Jesuit Fathers. They had a propaganda purpose. People read them in provincial châteaux and in the family circle in humbler homes, and the men and women who read them often decided as a result to go out to Canada. One of the stories that appealed to them most was the one about Hertel's captivity among the Iroquois, but since they had to be edifying the Jesuit Fathers didn't tell the whole story. François de Hertel was captured by the Iroquois who took him back to their village. As he put up a very brave fight, the Indians decided to torture him: they greatly admired courage and this was their way of rewarding a brave enemy. After all, there is a kind of logic about this Indian concept of how bravery should be recognized. The first thing they did was to burn the tips of his fingers in the bowl of a calumet. Poor Hertel suffered agonies but had strength enough not to cry out. Still, as he himself said in his letter to Father Le Moyne, he wasn't at all anxious to die as he wasn't in a state of grace and was afraid of appearing before God with a number of unconfessed sins on his soul. He was saved at the very last moment and for no other reason than that he was a good-looking young man. He was never so thankful for his looks as on this one vital occasion. A young Indian girl, who had watched him being tortured, had been moved, not by pity, which is a feeling unknown to the Indians, but by love. Now it was a custom among the Iroquois, who had some pretty curious ones, that a woman could save a prisoner by marrying him. The Indian girl said she wanted the

French Canadian and he was handed over to her without more ado."

My father read me extracts from Hertel's letters in the *Relations*: "Father, bless, I beseech you, the hand which writes and which has suffered the loss of a finger burnt in a calumet. . . . Do not let my mother know of this." Another letter, signed Fanchon and addressed to his mother, used to bring tears to my eyes. "You see," my father would say, "these letters took a long time to reach their destination. They were written on strips of birch-bark and given to the Indian girl who agreed to take them to the Jesuit mission. Hertel must have managed to make the Iroquois girl fall very much in love with him, but love is blind, with Indian girls just as with more civilized people. The poor girl made a mistake in delivering her lover's letters, because it meant that people in Quebec found out where he was being held. A party of French Canadians attacked the Indian village and Hertel was set free. When he left, did he look back even once at the woman whose love had saved him from the stake? I'm not sure he did, and I'm inclined to think he left in a hurry. What must this poor girl have thought of the man she loved? The same, I suppose, as all women think when they have been left in the lurch. You can be sure she shed a good many tears, but if she had had to do it all over again, she would have rescued him from the stake just as she had before. Women are always letting love get the better of them; it must be their generous nature that inspires them to act in this way.

"François de Hertel married a young French girl who had been sent out by the King to get herself a husband in the colony. She was called Mademoiselle de Thavenet and was the daughter of Raymond de Thavenet, an officer in the Régiment de Brinon. Their son, called Rouville, grew up to be a redoubtable warrior. As for François de Hertel, he lived to a great age, and the Abbé de Charlevoix, who saw him in 1720, wrote that he was revered as a hero throughout the colony. He had indeed led his men in many engagements, whether against the Indians or the English, and he was covered with scars. But perhaps when he glanced at his hands, with their missing fingers burnt off in a calumet in days gone by, he remembered his ghastly sufferings with a touch of tenderness. It must have reminded the old soldier too of one of his greatest triumphs, his conquest of the heart of a woman of the Iroquois."

The green folders each had a name. There was the Roquebrune folder, the Hertel folder, and the Salaberry folder. In this last one there was a portrait in among the papers. It was the likeness of a man in the uniform of a British general. It was done in crayon and had faded so much that it was very hard to make out. There was a black wooden frame and a glass to protect the picture and it was tied up in a bundle of letters from Edouard-Alphonse de Salaberry. These letters were from England. I asked my father who the man in the picture was.

He picked it up and turned it over and showed me a name written in ink. "Read it," he said. I studied the inscription carefully and spelled it out: "His Royal Highness the Duke of Kent." "Yes," my father said, "the Duke of Kent. And all these letters that Edouard de Salaberry wrote to his parents were sent from England. Some of them are dated from Kensington Palace when he was a guest of the Duke's. He was still little more than a child in 1808 when these letters were written; he was sixteen. The very short life of this young Salaberry had a touch of enchantment about it, but it ended in tragedy and death. Some natures have a grandiose destiny like that.

"The Irumberry de Salaberrys were shipbuilders in St. Jean-de-Luz, but a branch of the family lived in Paris and were quite well-to-do. In Louis XV's reign, a Salaberry was President of the Court of Exchequer, and Salaberry de Benneville was Admiral of the Western Ocean. The Abbé de Salaberry had been secretary to Cardinal de Polignac and was later chaplain to the Countess of Toulouse.

"The French branch of the family, which had influence at court, were able to be of help to their Basque cousins. That was why Michel de Salaberry, who had been a captain in the merchant service, became a naval officer and was able to derive all sorts of benefits from the Admiral's protection. Finally he sailed for Canada in command of *Le Chariot Royal*. In Quebec, French naval officers were always made welcome in the best homes, and whenever a ship of war docked there was always a round of receptions and dinners. Salaberry was made so very welcome that he married a young Quebec girl, a Rouer de Villeray. Then, a few weeks later, the captain sailed off again in his ship. By the time he came back again, two years later, his wife was dead, leaving a little daughter behind her. So Salaberry married another Quebec girl, a Juchereau de Saint-Denis, but he was still subject to the call of duty in the shape of the King's commands. While on a cruise with his squadron, he became involved in a naval engagement with the British, and he and his crew were captured and taken to England. By the time he got back to Quebec again, his wife was

waiting with a little son that had been born to them. In 1758, Salaberry was in command of *La Fidèle* and was sent to Louisbourg in
the squadron of Admiral Count Desgouttes. Boscawen, the British
Admiral, was attacking the fortress, which was defended by the
stout-hearted Chevalier de Drucour. Every morning, Madame de
Drucour climbed up to the ramparts and fired off a gun at the
British fleet. General Amherst got to hear of this and sent the brave
woman a basket of fruit. The whole population of Louisbourg, in-
cluding the garrison and Desgouttes' sailors, were starving to death
in the besieged city. Madame de Drucour sent her thanks to General
Amherst by a French-Canadian officer who went out in a rowboat
with a hamper of champagne for the British commander. The
General returned the compliment with still more fruit. 'Monsieur
Amherst seems very fond of champagne,' Monsieur de Drucour
remarked, 'but he's stripping my cellar.' So this time Madame de
Drucour sent the British General a flower."

My father rummaged about in the folder and took out a sheet of
paper. "Orders to Monsieur de Salaberry to scuttle his ship in the
narrows," he read. "It was Admiral Desgouttes and the Chevalier de
Drucour who signed these orders in the hope of preventing the
British fleet from sailing in through the narrows to Louisbourg.
Salaberry scuttled *La Fidèle*, but the sacrifice of his ship didn't save
the town and it had to surrender. Salaberry was sent off to England
as a prisoner along with the Drucours, Count Desgouttes, the garrison of Louisbourg and the sailors of the squadron. After the British
Conquest of Canada, *La Fidèle*'s commander was sent back to
France, and there he was joined by his wife and their little boy, who
was called Louis. In 1765, this Louis de Salaberry, who was only
thirteen at the time, left France and came back to Canada. His
parents had died at Rochefort leaving their orphaned son properties
near Quebec. So he came back to the colony, which had now become
a British possession. His sister was living there too at the time. She
had taken the veil with the Sisters of Mercy and was known as
Mother Geneviève d'Irumberry. Apart from this property, the boy
had no other possessions and, apart from his sister, the nun, no
other relatives. Louis de Salaberry grew up to be a magistrate and,
in 1793, was elected a member of the first Parliament of Canada. He
had already married Catherine de Hertel. This descendant of a long
line of sea-dogs turned out to be a sedentary, studious, serious-
minded sort of fellow. He lived in his little manor-house at Beauport

and spent the winters in Quebec. The most exciting thing that ever happened to him was a journey he made to France. Though they were British subjects now, the French Canadians had by no means renounced their abiding affection for their Mother Country nor their respect for 'the King.' Salaberry was presented to good King Louis XVI, and had the honour of kissing the hand of Queen Marie Antoinette and of watching the Dauphin playing in the Tuileries. His sponsor at court was the Salaberry who was president of the Court of Exchequer. The Revolution, when it came, filled Louis de Salaberry with revulsion. He just couldn't bring himself to believe that a people like the French whose civilization he admired so much, could make the guillotine the symbol of liberty.

"The Salaberrys did a lot of entertaining in Quebec. In fact their salon was the hub of fashionable life in the capital. People like the Lanaudières were received there as well as the Gaspés, the Hertels, the Panets, Monseigneur Bailly de Messein, and the Abbé Desjardins. French *émigrés* who had taken refuge in Canada were very welcome guests too and included people like the Saint-Aulaires, the Chalus, and the Marquis Du Barail. There were also English guests to be met with, and among them all, French or English, the most outstanding were the Countess de Saint-Laurent and the Duke of Kent.

"The presence in Quebec of the royal Duke and of his mistress, Madame de Saint-Laurent, had given rise to a good deal of gossip. People felt honoured and at the same time shocked by the fact that the Duke and the Countess had chosen Quebec as the place to flaunt their liaison. The Salaberrys put everybody at their ease by receiving the couple quite openly. After all the Duke of Kent was a son of the King and that altered circumstances a good deal. Besides Alphonsine de Montgenet-Fortison, Countess de Saint-Laurent, was both beautiful and charming, and it would have been difficult to refuse to entertain so delightful a person. The two struck up a close friendship with the Salaberrys and, when a child was born to the latter, in 1792, the Duke of Kent and Madame de Saint-Laurent insisted on standing as godparents. It was a boy and they gave him their two names; he was christened Edouard-Alphonse. They took a great liking to the child and became very closely attached to him. When the Duke of Kent was recalled to England in 1806, young Salaberry, who was fourteen then, went over to stay with him. His three older brothers were already officers in the British army, and the Duke got young Edouard a cadetship at the Royal Military College at Woolwich. In 1807, it happened that all four of the Salaberry brothers were in England at the same time. During his holidays, Edouard stayed with the Duke. The letters he wrote home to his parents give some account of his brilliant but all too brief career.

"It's all summed up in a few pages. On May 8, 1808, he wrote: 'I arrived at Kensington Palace this morning from Woolwich. I should have got here last night to accompany His Royal Highness to the Opera, but my captain would not grant me leave.' In another letter he wrote: 'I am spending the holidays with His Royal Highness. Madame de Saint-Laurent made me a present of a gold watch and has had a new suit of clothes made for me. I went driving with the Duke in his carriage in Hyde Park and then dined at Madame de Saint-Laurent's. The Prince of Wales was there and the Duke of Clarence and the Duke of Orléans. General Dumouriez was also among the guests; I found him an ugly little old man.' The Salaberrys were justified in believing that their son had begun his career in promising fashion and that it was likely to prove a brilliant one. Alas! The last of Edouard de Salaberry's letters is filled with dire presentiment. It was addressed to the Duke of Kent himself and dated 1812. The young man was twenty by this time and was serving as an officer in the British Army. Napoleon and the British were at war. The young lieutenant was encamped with his regiment in front of Badajoz, in Spain. One evening he sat down and wrote the Duke as follows: 'Your Royal Highness, I have been ordered to attack tonight. It may be that I shall not survive, and I wish to assure Your Royal Highness, and also Madame de Saint-Laurent, that, happen what may, I shall never forget what I owe you both.' "

My father stopped reading. He put down the last letter in the bundle, and though I knew the end of the story well, as I had heard it so often, I always asked, "What happened next?" Before replying, my father tied up Edouard de Salaberry's letters and put them back in the folder. "What happened next? Why, nothing. He was killed in the assault just a few hours after writing the letter I've just read you. The godson of the Duke of Kent and Madame de Saint-Laurent was soon just another British corpse rotting under the walls of Badajoz. That was the end of the career of Edouard de Salaberry."

He closed the folder, relit his pipe, and took a few puffs at it before continuing. "As for the Duke and Madame de Saint-Laurent, the death of the boy they were so fond of seems to have been the prelude to their parting. The Duke of Kent was forced for reasons of state to marry a princess, and that meant that he had to leave the woman he loved. In a way, Madame de Saint-Laurent and Edouard de Sala-berry were the wife and the son that the Duke of Kent would have liked to have. They were the protagonists in a single long-drawn-out romantic episode that gave his life its touch of poetry."

Before I ever read novels or stories, I was reared on these tales of the past, and these dramatic events of bygone days, in which my ancestors had played a part, made history especially real for me.

The old house where I was born and spent my childhood was saturated with the past. Everything in it and about it was a reminder of people who had been dead for many years. Their pictures, their furniture, and other objects which had belonged to them kept their vanished world alive.

A house, after all, can have its own mystery, its own secrets, and life and death both left their mark under this roof. Did the dead who once lived there ever return?

I believe that those who lived in the manor-house did return. One room in particular was their special preserve, and their silent pre-sences seemed to people it. Perhaps it was because so many of them died in that room. We always referred to it as "the room." The Chevalier de Saint-Ours and President Viger, the two husbands of our great-grand-aunt, both breathed their last in it, and, when her turn came, the seigneuresse died there too, as did my grandfather the Colonel. The last on the list was my brother, who lay ill in that room for many months before he died. Afterwards it was always kept locked. My mother was afraid of it and did her best to avoid it.

At nightfall, I used to be afraid of meeting ghosts in the upstairs corridors: Uncle Saint-Ours with his white wig and the satin bow at the nape of his neck, the Colonel leaning on his stick, my little brother propped up on his crutches, or even the seigneuresse. What were those vague noises in the corridor? They sounded like muffled voices, a murmured snatch of conversation, the gentle rustle of a silk petticoat, a light footfall. . . . There was a door standing ajar. Had it been opened by an invisible servant for Monsieur de Saint-Ours, who never opened doors himself? Was that my grandfather in his last agony or my little brother still gasping in pain in the huge bed?

The memory of their son and his illness was so painful to my parents that it was never mentioned in their presence, but I often heard from Sophronie about his prolonged suffering and his death. The old servant had known all the others too, years before: the Chevalier de Saint-Ours, President Viger, their wife the seigneuresse, and Colonel de Salaberry. She always referred to them by their titles, which stood for their actual persons in her mind and helped her to remember what they looked like, but, when she spoke about the Chevalier or the President or the Colonel or the seigneuresse, I always thought of them as characters in some old comedy and of her as the only one still living of those who had seen it played.

I remember the house where I was born as having a mysterious fascination. When I think of its big roof with the dormer windows, its rooms and their furniture, I think at the same time of my father and mother, my brothers and sisters and the servants, and in my memory their faces are interspersed with vague shadows, the familiar, friendly ghosts that haunted the old house.

One of my brothers had been an invalid since childhood, and no one knew what was the matter with him. The doctors knew far too little to be able to find out. Kind old Dr. Forêt called it "a bone disease." When he was seven my brother fell off his horse and from that time forward his back and his legs hurt him and he lay stretched out, pale and speechless, in his bed, or limped about painfully with the aid of a crutch or a stick.

My parents were heart-broken at their son's illness. My mother scarcely ever stopped praying and reciting the Rosary and lighting candles before the statue of St. Anne. In those days, St. Anne was still the great miracle-worker of French Canada. She seems to have declined a little in favour since then, though I have no idea why.

My parents thought the saint would be more likely to listen to them if they went to pray at her shrine at St. Anne de Beaupré, which had been a famous place of pilgrimage even in the old days when Canada was a French colony. So they set off with their son, full of faith and hope. The journey by carriage was a painful ordeal for the boy, but he loved the trip down the St. Lawrence in one of the paddle-wheel steamers of the Richelieu Navigation Company. The trip from Montreal to Quebec took the three pilgrims relatively few hours, and then they had to put up in a hotel to let the sick boy rest. Another carriage took them to the shrine at St. Anne de Beaupré. They were quite overcome when they saw all the crutches hanging in clusters and all the marble tablets engraved with the thanks of those for whom a miracle had been performed. They were quite sure that they too would be granted a miracle.

How distressed my parents were when they came back from their pilgrimage without any change in my brother's condition. These three had been so confident when they left, so sure that St. Anne could and would effect a miraculous cure. Nowhere were there three persons more deserving of a miracle. They were souls of uprightness and their hearts were as pure as one could wish. They would have accepted a miracle quite simply and without much surprise, but no miracle took place.

My mother was quite resigned and her faith was not in the least disturbed by the saint's apparent disregard for her prayers. As for the poor little sick boy, he finally died, clutching his Rosary and his holy medals in his thin, bony fingers. But my father, for his part, bore something of a grudge ever afterwards against Heaven for having remained deaf to his prayers. He maintained the rather injured dignity of someone who has had no reply to a letter he has written to an important person. In a way, my father seemed to think that Heaven had been somewhat lacking in courtesy.

So one day, when a member of the family suggested that he pray for the intercession of Venerable Mother d'Youville, who was a great-grand-aunt of his, my father replied somewhat tartly: "I hardly think where God's own grandmother has failed my great-grand-aunt would be likely to be more successful."

"We'll have to get Saint-Germain to come."

When anybody used that particular phrase, it meant there was a sick person in the house, and a sick person whom Dr. Forêt had been unable to cure. Official medicine in the person of Dr. Forêt looked with complete disapproval on Saint-Germain, while the clergy, represented by Father Dorval, practically consigned him to hell. The fact is that Saint-Germain, in spite of his cures, was not a regular doctor, and, in spite of his name, was very far from being a saint, but he had quite a reputation as a healer and a bit of a witch-doctor all up and down L'Assomption County. The habitants would call him in to cure a wife who had "a pain somewhere" or a child afflicted with St. Vitus' dance. He was also in great demand for cows that were "down sick" or for an old father who had "a growth." These were all complaints that came within the province of a healer. Their causes were mysterious and only a sort of medicine-man could deal with them properly. Saint-Germain was often able to help in cases where neither the doctor nor the priest seemed to understand what was the matter, for Saint-Germain was in his element with sick people or sick animals.

In those days there were healers and witch-doctors in every county in the province of Quebec. Initiates of this mysterious confraternity were to be found all up and down the St. Lawrence. I've met them myself on the banks of the Richelieu, in the fishing villages of the Gaspé Peninsula, and in the back blocks of Charlevoix County. They all looked rather alike and had the same sort of names, as if in some way they were all related. And they not only had the same cast of appearance; they even had almost identical traits. They were always old and bent like Saint-Germain. They had long, thin, pale faces, grey eyes, and those hooked noses which seem indispensable in their profession, and, even though they weren't all called Saint-Germain, they had the sort of names that linked them to the other healers in the province. These surnames were originally nicknames. There was, for example, a La Jeunesse who lived near Les Eboulements and a colleague of his called Saint-Maurice in the neighbourhood of Murray Bay. I once caught a glimpse of the local healer at St. Jean-Port-Joli, on the south shore of the St. Lawrence, and he was called L'Espérance. In the country around Rimouski there was a healer called Saint-Antoine, who covered all the territory from Pointe-au-Père to Notre Dame du Portage. The man in the Matepédia Valley was called Vadeboncœur and, in the valley of the Richelieu, Bon Courage. I knew a Sans Chagrin who lived on one of the islands off Boucherville and a Sans Peur who had a house on the lake of Two Mountains. The soldiers who served in the regiments that came out from France in the days of Count Frontenac and the Marquis de Vaudreuil had exactly the same names, names that belonged originally to marines, or to privates in the Régiment de Carignan, which was settled in the colony by Colbert. The healers of the province of Quebec, like all other French Canadians, were the descendants of men who had served in the armies of Louis XIV and Louis XV.

Their skill is almost forgotten today and the profession itself has more or less died out. Both human beings and animals seem to get along now somehow without their spells and their medicines. The country people don't believe in magic any more. They get the doctor in for a sick wife or the veterinary for a sick cow, and this has meant that some rather picturesque terms have passed out of current usage. French Canadians no longer talk about healers and casters of spells. These expressions, which were originally perjorative, and which had a recondite meaning too, no longer mean anything at all, and so they have dropped out of the language used by ordinary people.

The remedies these healers used came down to them from the Middle Ages. The principal ingredients in their pharmacoepia were plants and the blood of animals and fire and water. When these were administered they were accompanied by certain words and sacramental gestures. There was something of the prophet and the astrologer about them, and they still preserved traces of mediaeval lore going back to Albert the Great and the prophecies of St. Malachy and Nostradamus. The traditional science of the French-Canadian witch-doctors stemmed from all the provinces of France and it had been enriched by the contributions Indian medicine-men had made to it. So Saint-Germain and Bon Courage and Sans Chagrin and Vadeboncœur could lay claim to an illustrious lineage; their profession was as old as mankind itself.

"We'll have to get Saint-Germain to come."

Big Sophronie made that remark in the same tone that she might have used to say, "We'll have to go and get some sugar down at Archambault's." To the old woman's way of thinking, Saint-Germain's skill was just as necessary a commodity as Archambault's groceries. She well knew that Saint-Germain could effect cures that no doctor would dare to hope for. She had seen him at work, out on the farms, with his human and animal patients. His art left the science of the doctors far behind.

The first warm breezes had started. Out in the garden everything seemed to be dripping with moisture. A diaphanous haze of green buds had appeared on the elms that lined the drive. The water in the little river had risen from the melting snow and now tugged at the branches of the willows along the bank. Sambo left the door of the hen-roost open and no longer had to worry about the eggs getting frozen. As we sat about in the evenings after supper, the fragrance of the April night was wafted into the kitchen.

The Negro was of the same mind as Big Sophronie. He knew too that healers could be especially effective in the case of certain illnesses. He had seen them at work among the coloured folk of Virginia and Louisiana. He knew what a witch-doctor could accomplish with his incantations, or the blood of a rooster, or a concoction of herbs and flowers gathered at midnight when the moon was full.

"The trouble is," said Sophronie, "Mademoiselle won't like it."

She almost always called my mother Mademoiselle for she couldn't get used to calling her anything else.

Godefroy didn't much care for Saint-Germain and used to accuse him of hexing. Still he did go to fetch him once when Jess had a sore leg. The mare was limping and seemed to be in pain. My father and Godefroy looked her over and felt her leg, but couldn't find out where the trouble was. Jess wouldn't eat, her coat had lost its sheen, and she kept shivering all over. Then the healer came and took a look at her. He ran his fingers painstakingly all up and down her leg until he found the sore spot and the mare whinnied. Saint-Germain came back several times. He always wore a long black overcoat with its pockets stuffed with bottles. When he went into the stable he insisted that he be left alone with Jess. Godefroy grumbled a good deal. "That darn faker will kill the mare yet with his bag of tricks." But Saint-Germain didn't kill Jess. One day, as he was leaving, he said to Godefroy, "Your mare's all right now." And so she was, and even Godefroy had to admit it. Though he didn't like the healer, he respected his ability.

"Seeing he cured the mare," he said, "it's a sure thing he can cure Monsieur Léonide."

My mother had two brothers. René was younger than she and Léonide a few years older. Léonide and my mother were children of the first marriage, or "of the first bed," to use the French legal expression. René, Aunt Thérèse, and Aunt Alice were children "of the second bed." As I often heard this explanation given of the relationship of my mother to her brothers and sisters, my grandfather Salaberry's first and second beds assumed a rather odd genealogical significance for me, and a bed became something to do with ties of kinship.

Léonide de Salaberry and my mother both grew up in the manorhouse under the care of their grand-aunt the seigneuresse. When the old lady died, my mother and her brother inherited her fortune between them. What people called fortunes in those days wouldn't impress us much today, but in 1882 sixty thousand "bucks" was quite a legacy. The dollar was worth a great deal more and you could buy a great many things for very little money. Families lived in comparative luxury on an income that would strike us as wretched. Investments didn't add up to very big totals and could be quickly appraised. Léonide could consider himself comfortably well off. He was about thirty at the time. There was a photograph of him on the mantelpiece

C

in Mother's bedroom and it showed a tall, fair-haired young man with a pleasant expression. He wore a flower in his buttonhole and was leaning on a Malacca cane. His Christian name—Léonide—and this half-faded picture are all that remain of him in my memory. There are people like that, people who leave nothing behind but a quaint, out-moded name and a faded snapshot.

In the Montreal of the 1880's, he was just another easy-going young man about town. It is hard to imagine now what the place was like in those days. Some of the city streets were really no more than country roads. Each house stood in its own "yard." There were wooden sidewalks and the main thoroughfares were planted with trees on either side like the avenues of a park. Everybody knew everybody else and there was a lot of entertaining. In winter, when the Carnival was on, there were at least two or three balls a week. The Governor General always gave a big one, and that was the social event of the season. Sleighs with their buffalo-robes flying and their bells jingling glided along between two walls of ice. Nothing was ever done to remove the white carpet of snow from the streets, and after every blizzard the City Council had to mark out the roads afresh. The whole city seemed to sink deeper and deeper into the snow. In front of every house there was always a huge bank of it between the sidewalk and the roadway. Passages had to be dug here and there to give people a chance to get through. The popular winter sports were snowshoe parties and tobogganing on the slopes of the Mountain. In summertime, people played croquet in their yards. I imagine Léonide enjoyed himself as fully as was possible in those days.

But the question is: did he really confine his activities to playing croquet in peoples' yards and sliding down the Mountain on a toboggan? It may be that the young man who wore a flower in his buttonhole the day he had that yellowed picture taken was the victim of some great love-affair. What is quite clear is that at one point in his life he became completely absorbed in someone. He suddenly went off to England, and it must have been because he couldn't bear to be separated from the woman he loved. Some men fall in love so deeply that for them nothing has any real existence but the face and figure of their beloved. Léonide seems to have had a very tender heart, and people like that sometimes fall suddenly in love and remain constant in their affections for many years.

His relatives explained away his departure for England as an affectation. They knew he had a good many friends among the

English families in Montreal and assumed he had become hopelessly Anglophile. But relatives are often blind to the truth. What person in his right mind would go and spend years and years of his life in London just because he had a liking for things English? You can admire the English without having to go and live in England. In any case, it wasn't the English that Léonide had fallen in love with; it was an Englishwoman.

He used to write my parents from England two or three times a year, and my father read the letters out loud after dinner. Léonide was living in Mayfair and spoke about life in London with great enthusiasm. He seemed to find everything delightful. He went to the theatre a lot and was entertained a good deal too. As far as we could gather, he was enjoying it all immensely and his social vanity seemed comfortably inflated. However, gradually the tone of his letters changed. He complained of his health in winter when it became foggy and he couldn't stand the rain. He began to write nostalgically about those crisp, clear days in January when the sun and the snow are blindingly bright. He became sentimental about the streets of Montreal with their snowbanks. Once he wrote that he had made friends with a Frenchman just to have the pleasure of speaking his own language and particularly of hearing it. After a while he began to write very critically about the English way of life and people in London. He harped especially on English customs and systems of heating. He had taken a dislike to tea and to marmalade and absolutely refused to eat any more roast beef. His relatives concluded that he no longer loved the English. But it wasn't the English that he no longer loved; it was an Englishwoman.

A soft April sun shone on the garden and warmed the walls of the house. As the carriage turned in the far end of the drive, it passed between the two green-painted balls that guarded the entrance to the property. Léonide looked about him with that curiosity you feel on returning to a familiar place that you have almost forgotten after a long absence. It is all just as it was and yet somehow different. You imagined the house was bigger and the garden too, but it is the people most of all who make you realize the passage of time.

My mother came out on to the doorstep to welcome the returning traveller. My father got down from the carriage and held out both hands to Léonide, who seemed to have some difficulty in getting out of the seat. He finally managed, but it obviously cost him an effort, and when he crossed our threshold he was limping and leaning heavily on my father's arm. Mother was very much upset and at once wanted to know why he couldn't walk properly. Léonide tried to reassure her by telling her there was nothing wrong with him, but obviously there was something wrong.

He was put in the west bedroom at the end of the upstairs corridor. Léonide seemed delighted to be back in the bosom of the family with everybody making a fuss over him. After all the years spent in England among strangers, it was a joy to be back in the old house and to take up the old ways again. The green arm-chair next to the fireplace, the curtains on his windows, the view over the tops of the trees, the sound of Mother's voice downstairs—all these things made him feel he had come home and seemed to wipe away a whole stretch of his life he wanted to forget. Imagine going so far in search of happiness when perhaps it is to be found in the furniture of a familiar room or in a garden where you know every pathway by heart! He just didn't want to think any more about the cause of his unhappiness, but though he had left London for good, he was never quite able to forget Mayfair.

Dr. Forêt came in to have a look at his leg. "It's rheumatism," he said, "caused by all that fog. The English all have trouble with this sort of thing because of the climate of the British Isles." He prescribed hot lemonade and plenty of rest, but these harmless remedies were hardly sufficient to cure the sickness that Léonide had contracted in the British Isles. He didn't seem to get any better.

"We'll have to get Saint-Germain to come."

Big Sophronie, who went up to Léonide's room every day, kept saying this over and over again. The old woman fussed about when she was up there, pulling the bed-covers straight or dragging the arm-chair in front of the window. She would help the sick man get his leg up on a cushion, which rested on a footstool, and when she had got him to drink a cup of her excellent coffee, she would leave the room muttering to herself that they would have to get the healer in. Sophronie played a very important part at the manor-house in all matters connected with food or sickness. This was her special domain, and nobody would have denied that she had had plenty of experience in these matters. My mother and Léonide had both been accustomed from childhood to paying attention to what she had to say. Léonide gulped down Sophronie's coffee while my mother finally agreed to consult Saint-Germain.

The healer lived between L'Assomption and St. Sulpice in a white-washed, frame house that stood back from the road behind a small garden. There was nothing at all sinister about it. Though there may have been strange herbs growing in the garden, their leaves looked perfectly normal, and, if the healer did concoct magic brews in his kitchen, he cannot have used any but the usual vegetables for that purpose. At his place, the witch's cauldron shared the stove with the stew-pot.

Godefroy brought him back one day when he had been on an errand to the village. Sophronie did Saint-Germain the honours of her kitchen and gave him a piece of pie and a cup of coffee. The old woman viewed all social contacts in terms of eating and drinking, and she considered it her duty to press food on people on every possible occasion. When he had finished, the healer went upstairs to see his patient. He examined the leg carefully, and as his long fingers probed the sore muscles there were one or two stifled cries of pain. He then took a small bottle out of his overcoat pocket and asked for a piece of flannel, insisting that it must be red. This was the beginning of the treatment. Saint-Germain came back a good many times, but Léonide still seemed to be in pain. Neither the massage he was given, nor the ointment, nor the red flannel seemed to make any difference. One evening, my father, who seemed baffled by it all, remarked, "I think Léonide will have to make up his mind to consult a specialist in Montreal." But they hadn't lost faith in Saint-Germain out in the kitchen. "He fixed up that cow at La Sloune's place last month," said Sophronie. Godefroy scratched his head and said, "Maybe he's a better hand with cows than with folks."

On one particular day, when Saint-Germain was supposed to come and treat his patient he didn't turn up. This seemed to be rather a bad sign, for Léonide wasn't any better and his leg still hurt him. It certainly looked as if the healer had given up. Godefroy was very angry. "I'll go fetch that no-good; it don't make sense leaving Monsieur Léonide in the lurch like that with a sore leg." When Godefroy turned up at the witch-doctor's place the latter was working in his garden. As soon as Godefroy opened his mouth to speak, he stopped him with a gesture. "Hold your tongue," he said. "It is written in the Scriptures that God will call men to account for the words they utter. Besides there was no point in my going back to your place. The man is cured." And so saying he turned his back on Godefroy and went on transplanting his lettuces.

As a matter of fact, Léonide was cured. He started walking up and down in his room the very next day, and he was able to come downstairs and have dinner with the rest of the family. Saint-Germain's spells or his massage had worked a miracle. My parents were rather surprised because they hadn't really believed in the healer. My mother was very pleased, of course, though a little disappointed that the cure should have been due to a healer's incantations. Probably Sophronie and Sambo were the only ones in the whole household who weren't in the least surprised, for the simple reason that they had never doubted that the healer and his arts would succeed; to them it was a perfectly natural happening. The world of miracles had its rightful place in the old woman's imagination and the world of mystery in the religious mind of the Negro.

I never met Uncle Léonide. By the time I was born he had left Canada again, but I was very inquisitive about him all through my childhood, perhaps because it struck me as very adventurous to be always going off to distant parts. This uncle who lived abroad became quite a romantic figure in my eyes. He was always referred to with bated breath and that only served to increase his prestige. Every time I was told a story about a young man driven by love to journey in faraway places, I always imagined Uncle Léonide as the hero.

He went to live in New York, though I never did find out why. Perhaps an American woman was responsible this time. Léonide's comings and goings always provoked a good deal of speculation, but what did this dreamer hope to find in the New York of 1890? Did he discover happiness on Broadway or 42nd Street? Those were the days when immense fortunes were being made in the United States, and quite a number of Canadians moved south of the border. Perhaps, as his income had been reduced by his long stay in England, Léonide dreamed of becoming rich. He had studied law at one time and my father advised him to practise his profession in Montreal. However, he chose to practise in New York instead. In the end he made a lot of money and became completely Americanized. One day he wrote to tell us he was married.

My mother was delighted by the news. Her ideas of a place like New York were confused and terrifying. She imagined her brother plunged into this infernal city where even the streets had no names, only numbers. A photograph of New York as it was in those days doesn't strike us as particularly infernal now. It looks rather like a country town with the streets full of horse-drawn vehicles. Down near Wall Street are a few fifteen-storey buildings. But then what little information my mother had about life in the United States made it all appear very frightening. After all, to someone who had lived all her life in the manor-house at L'Assomption, fifteen-storey buildings seemed pretty alarming. The fact that Léonide had married made him appear more human again. Presumably people who lived normal lives in New York didn't perch up on the top of fifteen-storey buildings. "They are just office buildings," my father said reassuringly. "Léonide probably lives in a two-storey house." And he added, "A house like one of those we saw in Boston."

My parents had been to Boston on their honeymoon. In 1874, that was really quite a journey. Canadian cities bore very little resemblance to American ones then, and as soon as you took the train for Massachusetts or Pennsylvania you were on your way to a totally different civilization. When my mother went to Boston, she learned what going abroad meant. The only thing she really liked there was a large park near the hotel where she went for walks in the evening arm-in-arm with her husband. She imagined that in New York Léonide must also enjoy losing himself in parks with his bride.

My parents were delighted with what Léonide had to say about her. She had a French name, Hortense Hébert, and was descended from a Louisiana family. She didn't sound at all American. It was a relief to know that Léonide, even after living in New York for so long, had married a girl with a name like Hortense Hébert. She came of seafaring stock apparently, and her father had been a ship's captain. Léonide went down to New Orleans to visit his parents-in-law. Hortense's grandmother still lived in a house in the French Quarter. "It's all very French down here," Léonide wrote, "as French as in the province of Quebec. Hortense's grandmother can't speak a word of English." Even as late as the end of last century, the French families of Louisiana still survived as a compact social group and had been very little affected by American influences. Their manners and customs were still those of the period before the Civil War and their great hero was still General Toutant de Beauregard.

Léonide never did come back to Canada. He went on practising law in New York and became more and more like an American business man. He even became naturalized and changed his name to "Mr. Salsberry." There are people like that who can shed their personalities completely when they leave their former surroundings. They turn into someone entirely different. Léonide not only became a different person; even his physical apprerance changed. New York is a place that can cast a strange spell on people, and it can transform them competely. Such a force is quite irresistible. If Napoleon Bonaparte were born again in New York, he would inevitably grow up to be a big business man with an office near Wall Street. Léonide didn't have a very strong character, and so New York changed him very quickly. About 1896, he sent my parents a photograph of himself. They looked at it with amazement. It was the picture of a man with a furrowed brow, a grim expression, and a hard look about the eyes that bore absolutely no resemblance to Léonide, and no wonder, for it was in fact a picture of Mr. Salsberry.

New York kills off its inhabitants ruthlessly, especially in summer during the great heat-waves. The dog-days are as dangerous as a full-scale epidemic, and people collapse on the sidewalks and in their offices. Crowds make their way out of the city to go and spend the night on the beaches, or they sleep in the parks—anything to get away from their oven-like apartments. The hospitals are crowded with half-demented victims of sunstroke or heatstroke, and the huge city turns into a sort of cauldron in which millions of human beings slowly melt in the intense heat.

It was during the dog-days that Léonide died. He was stricken as if an unseen enemy had hit him between the eyes and he collapsed unconscious in his office. The ordinary doctors could do nothing for him and, unlike L'Assomption, New York had no healer to offer him. New York's magic is of a different sort, and perhaps Léonide died because he never really found that out.

It was a very common occurrence for my father to spend the evening reading. He would sit quite motionless for hours at a time completely absorbed in his book. Near by, Mother went on with her sewing in the circle of light cast by the lamp. The profound silence in the room was only broken by the occasional rustle of a turning page. I can remember all this so vividly because it was such a familiar happening, and the setting I always associate it with is the corner of the dining-room over near the big stove in winter. We were usually all three of us rather drowsy from the heat.

My brothers and sisters studied their lessons and wrote out their exercises in a special workroom upstairs, and Mademoiselle Villeneuve was there every evening to keep an eye on them. If I did venture into their sanctum, Roquebrune would usually tell me to get out, and

René wouldn't even bother to look up. My presence disturbed the secret reading they indulged in behind the screen of their lesson-books. Jules Verne was their great favourite. Only occasionally did Mademoiselle Villeneuve spare them an absent-minded glance, and then she would quickly go back to her novel, for this sentimental governess was greatly addicted to love stories. Aline and Hervé were the only ones willing to let me stay a moment and listen to them reading aloud. They could rarely bring themselves to deny me any-thing, and so I would be treated to snatches of *Robinson Crusoe* or *Michael Strogoff* or *The Misfortunes of Sophie*. I didn't always understand what it was all about but I listened with rapt attention. Then my two oldest brothers would start to grumble again and to make it quite clear that I was in the way, and off I would go down-stairs feeling I had been cast out of paradise. Back in the dining-room, I would usually find my father reading a passage in a low voice to my mother, who sat with her head bent over her sewing. As she listened her dear face would suddenly light up with a charming smile.

By this time I usually felt I had been shut out from a world whose secrets I could never penetrate and would go and take refuge in the kitchen. It was a sure bet that Sophronie and Sambo wouldn't be reading and perhaps they would take some notice of me.

Reading! What did it mean exactly to be able to read? I was much intrigued by this problem and for a long time it seemed quite in-soluble. I would pick up one of those things that grown-ups called a book and look at it full of wonder, turning over the pages. Think of all the magic locked up in it! I knew these black signs stood for people and what they said and what they did, and there were horses and animals and all sorts of things hidden away in all this print. I had heard my father read things out to my mother which she had found very moving, and on those occasions she would sometimes let her hand rest for a moment on his arm and say, "How beautiful!" or sometimes, "How true!"

One day I asked Mother what book it was he had been reading to her from, and she smiled and said, "It's a love story."

When we started off to Mass on Sundays everybody always carried a book with red edges to the pages, and in church I could see lots of people all round me reading out of the same sort of book. I had been told that these were prayer-books. And then the Abbé Dorval, when he was saying Mass, would walk up and down in front of the altar and bow and genuflect and cross himself and bless us only to go off suddenly to one side to read out of a big book propped up wide open at one end of the altar. He would lean over the book and mutter away in a strange language. Then he would start to intone in this same mysterious but musical tongue. I found all this very puzzling, but I had been told that the book on the altar was in Latin. What a lot of different things there seemed to be in books: love and people and the things they did and prayers and Latin! That is why, when I did pick up a book, I would always examine it with a mixture of anxiety and curiosity, thinking I might perhaps discover something in it all by myself.

But I always met with the same disappointment. Nothing happened. The book, as far as I was concerned, was mute and empty. I just didn't have the key to the treasure-house, but at least I knew the key existed and that I might get hold of it some day. Then first Jacques and later Mother started teaching me to read, and so I learned the great secret.

Jacques Simard was quite an educated person. So was his father for that matter, for though he was an habitant, he had taken the classical course at L'Assomption College, and Jacques had followed his example. In those days it was quite usual in country districts to come across unpretentious farmers who had studied the humanities. They had been through college and had then gone back to the land to follow in their fathers' footsteps.

Those old French-Canadian classical colleges, run by the priests, did exert a profound influence. Along with a little Latin and a little Greek they taught a whole way of life first conceived centuries ago along the sunlit shores of the Mediterranean. This ancient culture, which came to Canada with the first missionaries and the first colonists, managed to survive, and it was the country priests who kept the traditions alive. The fact that they had done some Latin and read some of the French classics left its mark on the French-Canadian peasantry. It wasn't at all unusual to meet a farmer who could quote Virgil or an habitant who used tag-ends of Corneille and Racine in his everyday speech.

Jacques read a great deal and owned books himself, a fact which, incidentally, made people in the village look at him rather suspiciously. People didn't think it was a very good thing for a young man to exhibit so much curiosity and to be so absorbed in books. Books were a source of error and even of evil-doing, veritable repositories of sin, as was well known. The parish priests were dead against

books and wouldn't allow people to read them. Every year the Abbé
Dorval preached a special sermon against bad books. "This thirst for
reading," he thundered, "is an idle form of curiosity and a dangerous
one. Be on your guard, my brethren; a bad book is often the doorway to Hell."

Jacques had noticed how anxious I was to learn to read, so he began
to teach me one evening when he dropped in, as he often did, to spend
an hour chatting in the kitchen. He was fond of those evenings with
the two Sophronies and Godefroy and Sambo and myself. These two
unlettered women, the man-of-all-work, the old Negro from the
United States, and the little boy seemed to constitute a group that
appealed to him. I wonder what secrets Jacques learned from us and
what special wisdom we were able to give to help him live the life he
had chosen. Perhaps these simple and straightforward people he used
to meet in the manor-house kitchen supplied him with something he
needed. In any case, what Big Sophronie or Sambo had to say was
every bit as well worth listening to as the talk of educated persons.

As a matter of fact, they were educated in their own way too. The
old cook and the old Negro both had a rich fund of experience, and
they could talk of life's problems, each in his or her own way, with
wisdom and discernment.

Whenever I knew Jacques was in the kitchen, I would rush out to
see him and climb up on his knee. He always sat at the big table in the
middle of the room, next to Godefroy, who leaned with his elbows
on the rough, worn surface smoking his pipe. Big Sophronie would
be washing the dinner dishes with Sambo drying. The dogs lay sleeping around the stove, and the cats, bunched up beneath it, purring,
watched us with aloof expressions.

The big kitchen was lighted by two oil lamps. One stood in the
middle of the big table and had a shade on it, and the other hung on
the wall next to the stove like a lantern. There were always deep
shadows here and there: in the far corners, near the three-piece
buffet, under the cupboards, along the baseboards, and between the
rafters of the low ceiling. In the evening, the big wooden arm-chairs,
which were pushed back along the wall in daytime, were dragged
around the table in the middle of the room.

And it was there, at the kitchen table, with Sophronie clattering
her dishes and Godefroy smoking his coarse, strong tobacco and
Sambo smiling at me as he put the dishes away—it was there that

Jacques one evening brought out a book and started to teach me to read. It was in the big, richly odorous kitchen, smelling of garlic and curdled milk, with the old, familiar friends of my childhood around me—the two Sophronies and Godefroy and Sambo—that I learned from Jacques the first principles of all knowledge and the beginning of learning, and it was through him that sin in its gravest but most delightful form began to take possession of my mind and corrupt my soul—the sin of curiosity.

There were quite a lot of books in the manor-house, which had all belonged to my grandfather. I remember the lovely, fawn-coloured, eighteenth-century bindings and the miniature format of the books of the post-Napoleonic period. A three-volume *Gil Blas* was to follow me through life, and I have preserved it piously. My father did absolutely nothing to add to this library; indeed, during the eighty-three years of his life, he never bought a single book. The French Canadians of his generation had lost the habit of reading, and the influence exerted by a certain Bishop of Montreal was responsible in no small measure for persuading people that books were the invention of the Devil. This bishop excommunicated, in other words condemned to hell-fire, the members of a literary society called the Institut Canadien because these members read "bad books." This bishop had the soul of an inquisitor. In all other respects he was a saintly person and was profoundly venerated by the faithful of the Diocese of Montreal.

These episcopal fulminations made a considerable impression on my father, and in our family the words "bad books" were not treated lightly. As nobody bought any books of any sort, no bad books ever came into the house, and my grandfather's books in their handsome bindings stood undisturbed for many years in their shelves in the bookcase, the poison distilled by bad authors still potent in their guilty pages. Voltaire and Diderot were among those present and Jean-Jacques and the Encyclopaedists. One day, the Abbé Dorval, who had come to call, happened to glance at these rows of books and started back in horror. The demons of Free Thought and of the Higher Criticism stood ready to leap out of the bookcase. My father had laid himself open to the severest condemnation. What sort of an excuse was it to keep such books about the place simply because they had nice bindings? The soul of every member of the household was in mortal peril. Even Big Sophronie, who didn't know how to read, might be contaminated from coming into contact with books of this sort. The very sight of them was an occasion for sin, for they were capable of exerting a mysterious and diabolic power. Only fire could extirpate this malevolent influence, so my father was told that Voltaire and Diderot must be consigned to the flames.

The *auto-da-fé* took place in a corner of the garden and many were the books reduced to ashes that were afterwards buried in a hole in the ground. My father was quite convinced that by burning the books he had helped to wipe out error and defend the cause of religion.

His own choice of reading had never been in the slightest degree revolutionary. Unlike my grandfather, he wasn't inquisitive about ideas or easily caught up by them. It was no effort for him to conform. The books he liked to read best were rather dull, colourless, historical treatises.

My mother was by nature a romantic and was very partial to sentimental love stories, but they had to be strictly orthodox. To get the kind of books she wanted, she subscribed to a special Catholic collection which dealt in "edifying novels." Once or twice she dipped into one of Bourget's more harmless stories, but her anxiety not to overstep the strictest bounds of propriety made her recoil from this dangerous author.

Because of my parents' attitude, I really thought, until I was about fifteen, that there was a hidden wickedness in books. For that very reason I was intensely curious about them, and as soon as I could I began to read "bad books" with the greatest delight.

Sometimes, in the evening, the quiet of the garden was disturbed by a sudden thudding sound, a noise of beating wings and of a body falling through space, as if somebody or something had lost balance and had fallen on to the lawn.

It used to frighten me a little and I would listen anxiously. There was something very disquieting about this abrupt thud, like the sound of a violent though invisible catastrophe, the death-fall of a wandering spirit suddenly hurled to earth.

In actual fact, I knew perfectly well what caused this sound of rushing wings. It was the nightjar and had nothing to do with fallen angels or the souls of the departed.

I only managed to see this bird in the garden once or twice. It was quite a small creature. I never heard its curious wing-beats or its deep, plaintive sigh in the daytime, or if I did I never paid any attention then. I always think of it as happening in the evening, or just at nightfall.

My recollection of the sudden, plunging dive of the nightjar out in the garden is closely linked with my memories of the evenings of my childhood days.

What a strange thing the silence of the dead is! They seem no longer interested in earthly happenings. And if sometimes a departed spirit returns to wander in the place where it once lived, it does so with the greatest discretion. Only the vaguest indications betray its unwonted presence, so that the living are usually not aware of it.

The people who surrounded me in my childhood are all dead now, and only my recollection of them calls them back to life.

And yet, night, where the dead hold sway, sometimes brings one of them back from the remote, unknowable place where they dwell. When sound asleep and dreaming, I sometimes see them again. On such occasions my parents are all mixed up in a most unexpected way with places and people belonging to a totally different period of my life when they were no longer alive. The incoherent nature of dreams brings people and periods together in this way, disregarding time and space, and forming fresh groups by choosing from successive layers of memory.

Just the other day, I dreamed at one and the same time of my mother and of my home in Paris. I was in the big sitting-room up-stairs with some friends and Mother was there with us. She was in the easy-chair in the corner by the piano and was looking out at the terraces and the trees in the grounds of St. Perrine. Josée was there too and so were Cathelineau and Fleuriot de Langle. And there was still another presence there. At first I didn't want to go into the room and in the doorway I started back. I didn't want to see whoever it was who was there. I didn't want to hear that voice, because when I do, it is too painful. I made a great effort to escape from my dream and finally succeeded, for soon another dream took its place.

Sometimes too, I dream about the old house in L'Assomption. All the people I grew up among seem to be still there. My mother sits in the dining-room near the fireplace. Often my father seems not to be there, but I know he will come home soon. Sambo is out in the garden. I open a door and there is the staircase leading down to the kitchen. Big Sophronie beckons to me from where she stands behind the big table piled high with poultry and vegetables. Then I take another step forward and find myself suddenly in a street in Paris, just as if the house where I was born had been pulled down and put up again in the Rue Molitor.

The madness of dreams confuses and confounds everything. My mother never went to Paris in her life and never lived in my house in the xvith *arrondissement*. Yet, when I dream about my home in Auteuil, I often see her in it talking to those Parisian friends of mine she never knew. But perhaps it is difficult for the dead to find their way back to the places where they once lived. Only the people they loved, and who continue to think of them, can really draw them back. My memories of Mother bring her to me, and she takes advantage of my dreams to be with me again.

The dead must have to use all sorts of subterfuges to escape, if only for a moment, from their state and make contact with some loved one still in the world of the living. Probably the world of dreams is the only place where meetings of this sort, between the living and the dead, can really occur.

Part Three

❊

THE HAPPY HOME

My father was a happy-go-lucky sort of man and thoroughly good-tempered, but he was very alert, and had a dry sense of humour. Very occasionally he would fall into a fit of depression and have nothing to say for himself. This would generally happen when he had trouble with one of his tenant-farmers, or his house property in Montreal needed repairs, or somebody had walked off without paying the rent. But as a rule he didn't worry overmuch and took things in his stride. He was a first-rate conversationalist and used to keep us all amused. He was particularly good at taking people off with a single word or phrase or with the description of a trait that made them come suddenly alive even if it put them in a ridiculous light. It always made Mother laugh because she admired everything he said and did and was literally fascinated by him. However, as she was fundamentally a kind-hearted person, she used to scold him for making such fun of people. "Please don't talk like that. . . . They're full of good qualities and it isn't nice to make fun of them." My father would shrug his shoulders. "Good qualities indeed! My dear, the world is just swarming with men and women who are full of good qualities and that doesn't prevent them from being highly comical. I'm sure the Almighty meant them to be like that seeing he created them in the first place, and I'm inclined to think that he would be the first to laugh at them. After all, one way of showing respect for him is to recognize that the human beings he created have their amusing side.

72

I am sure it would flatter the pride he takes in his creation." Mother would look at him and say with a smile, "If making fun of people is a way of showing respect for the Creator, you must stand very high in his estimation."

When he came back from collecting his rents in Montreal, my father always had a fresh fund of amusing stories, and his remarks about this person or that, though often biting, were sprinkled with comical sidelights. His manner of speaking was always very forceful, and the French he used in these descriptions of his trips very correct, as was generally the case with French Canadians of his generation. The people he had seen, the drawing-rooms he had visited, or the houses where he had dined passed in a panorama before us. He usually talked about his trips to the city at dinnertime, for that was his favourite hour of the day. When he saw us all gathered around him it seemed to stimulate his imagination. We were, in fact, a perfect audience and were always delighted by everything he said. Sometimes, when the story was a little *risqué*, or his remarks rather too frank, Mother would make a sign to him. His liveliness and directness always made her a trifle nervous, and so sometimes she would interrupt him suddenly, saying in English, "Dear, don't speak that way before the children, please."

This was always a disappointment to us, because we knew it meant we weren't going to hear the end of the story, or that some rather daring tale would now never reach its proper climax. "Dear, don't talk that way before the children, please," meant that we would never find out why Madame X, who was a friend of my parents, had left Monsieur X, or that the story about Monsieur So-and-so, which had begun so amusingly, would never be finished. My father would stop short and, twirling the ends of his moustache, would give us a knowing look, as if to say, "You see, I can't help it, but it's a pity, because I was just coming to the really funny part."

"I met Monsieur Y," my father said on one occasion. "He's still using that extraordinary looking calf's head he calls a face."

"If poor Y didn't have his . . . well, the kind of head you say he has, you'd be pretty disappointed," Mother replied. "And you seem to use his head as if it were a Turk's head at a fair-ground—something to take pot-shots at."

"A Turk's head! For once your good nature has forced you to speak the truth without knowing it. I've always thought Y must have something of the Turk in him. He's as strong as a professional boxer and that's probably why the ladies all make up to him. As you know, he's a great success with them all, and quite a night-hawk too, and that Madame B, who has round heels, is supposed to be his. . . ."

"Please, dear, don't speak that way before the children," my mother said with a look of alarm.

So my father broke off what he was saying and started in on another story which had inevitably to be censored in its turn. He was quite incorrigible, and so all through dinner that stock English phrase kept coming in, "Please, dear, don't speak that way. . . ."

My father made use of all sorts of old French words, which were vigorous and colourful, and turns of speech which were still current in his day but which are now no longer heard. Sometimes I find myself using one of his expressions. *Partir comme un fusil sans plaque* meant to go off like a shot without saying good-bye properly. *Etre dos blanc* meant to be badly behaved, to have the manners of a hobbledehoy. *Cafouiller* was to stutter, to speak indistinctly. *La lettre en est bien grosse* referred to anything that was glaringly obvious. *Tornicoter* meant to pace up and down or fidget about for no apparent reason. *Baragouiner* was to speak French badly and mispronounce words. His own French was very precise and he had an extensive vocabulary. He used the old French-Canadian pronunciation, which was akin to that used in France in an earlier age. My father spoke as his father had spoken before him, as the French Canadians spoke long ago, that is to say admirably, and, like them, he had a taste for a good story, a spicy phrase, and the art of conversation.

Some of the expressions he used particularly struck me and I would ask him to explain them because I wanted to know what they meant. What did "being a night-hawk" mean? What kind of a lady was "a lady with round heels?" I had visions of a lady with big round bumps on her heels, and it seemed to me a very strange thing to have. I thought it might be a kind of malformation.

This latter phrase seems to have impressed me more than any other, and one evening at dinner I asked, "Mother, has Mademoiselle Le Prohon got round heels?"

My father guffawed loudly. Mademoiselle Le Prohon was a very respectable and rather straitlaced old lady of over sixty.

"I expect she'd like to have," said my father still convulsed with laughter. "I expect she'd like to have, but at her age it would be rather. . . ."

On that occasion we didn't hear the phrase, "Don't speak that way," because Mother was stifling her giggles in her serviette. The idea of accusing the venerable Mademoiselle Le Prohon de Beaufort of having "round heels" conjured up an association of words and images that proved quite irresistible. It made Mother forget all her English and finally sent her off into such peals of laughter that she was soon gasping for breath.

Sometimes my father would sing to us. We could always hear him warbling to himself in his room when he got dressed in the morning, and he would practise scales or try out snatches of song when he went to visit the horses in the stable, while Godefroy was grooming them, or watched Sambo stacking the winter cordwood in the shed. He was always off key, as he was the first to admit, but that didn't prevent him from treating us to periodic concerts of his own special kind.

Like some of the expressions he used, his favourite songs were inclined to be spicy—very "French," to say the least. He had an enormous repertory of them: old guardroom ditties he had learned from his father or from his uncle La Broquerie, old army songs from Montcalm's day, that Canadian soldiers had sung around the camp-fires of the Monogahéla and Carillon, drinking songs that had been popular in officers' messes in the Seven Years' War or the War of 1812, songs of the Rebellion of 1837 that his grandfather had taught him, patriot songs that Roquebrune had hummed to himself as he blazed away at the British during the battle of St. Denis on the Richelieu, songs of colonial days that were sung when Canada was still called New France.

In one long ditty each verse ended with the refrain *C'est la faute à Papineau*. This was the song of the French-Canadian insurgents of 1837. Those men who fought so bravely in the battles along the Richelieu and the Lake of Two Mountains had bawled it out at the tops of their lungs as they loaded their muskets. He was also very fond of Etienne Cartier's song *O Canada, mon pays, mes amours*. The patriots had sung it in their prison cells. Another favourite of his was *Un Canadien errant, banni de ses foyers*. This had been the special song of the exiles, of the French Canadians who were transported to Australia or Bermuda. But though he was especially fond of these "tunes" associated with a particular and tragic event in our past history, he really very much preferred spicy, eighteenth-century soldiers' songs. Some of them were really hair-raising. I never got to know them properly because he always left out the more shocking verses and all we really heard were bits of the chorus. I can only remember one, of which he seemed particularly fond, because he was always humming it. This great masterpiece finished with:

> *Oh! c'te dinde*
> *Elle ne savait pas*
> *Que dans les Indes*
> *On faisait caca.* . . .

Whenever my father stopped telling stories or comparing people to barnyard animals or kitchen utensils, when he no longer used *risqué* expressions and sang songs, when he had hardly a word to say for himself, then we knew that things were going badly and that he was worried and ill-at-ease about something. When this happened, he would remain silent for long periods of time and would seem lost in meditation. He took no part in the general conversation at table. We would all fall a prey to sadness then, and a wave of melancholy would spread through all the house. My mother would look very worried as she glanced surreptitiously at her husband. She usually knew what was bothering the person she loved best in the whole world; her tender, wifely heart would suffer at the thought and her face would grow pale.

But as soon as the crisis passed, and the financial difficulties had been set right again somehow or other, then my father would join in the talk around the dining-table again, and would start telling amusingly malicious stories about his acquaintances, interspersed with somewhat improper remarks. And when he could be heard in his bedroom or out in the stable singing *Un Canadian errant* or *Oh! c'te dinde*, then Mother's smile would return and she would become a happy and contented person once again. On those occasions if, from sheer force of habit, she started to interrupt with, "Dear, don't speak that way," she would check herself abruptly. After all, she was really glad to have him tell his stories since it was a proof that his happiness had returned.

My parents weren't particularly enthusiastic about seeing people, whether they had to entertain guests or go visiting themselves. They were completely self-sufficient, and their rather isolated existence in the manor-house had confirmed their taste for solitude. I have never known any two persons who were so completely uninterested in making new friends. They lived very much as they pleased, and all they asked was to be left alone.

Still, people did occasionally come to stay and there were casual visitors too. Many families living in L'Assomption and the neighbouring villages were on calling terms. There was a certain amount of social life in that part of the world and a good deal of visiting back and forth.

Marriages and funerals were always the occasion for a substantial banquet.

When the nuptial mass was over, the blushing bride, clinging to the arm of her bridegroom in his frock-coat and top-hat, would come back to her parents' home for the wedding breakfast. Relatives appeared from St. Sulpice and Repentigny and Montreal, their rigs lined up in the yard. The horses would be unharnessed and led out to the stable. Then the meal would begin as soon as the Abbé Dorval, Notary Le Mire, and Dr. Forêt had arrived.

These three worthies were the guests of honour at every wedding breakfast, for after all they were the three official personages most closely concerned. It was Notary Le Mire's job to draw up the marriage contract, the Abbé Dorval performed the ceremony and, within the year, Dr. Forêt completed the cycle by delivering the young wife of her first-born. These three gentlemen usually met at funerals as well, and here again there was official justification for their presence, for Notary Le Mire had drawn up the deceased's will, Dr. Forêt had looked after him in his last illness, and the Abbé Dorval had buried him.

The functions they exercised invested them with a good deal of prestige. Notary Le Mire was a little old man with white hair and a goatee, who wore gold-rimmed spectacles. The Abbé Dorval's large blue eyes gave him an expression of great candour, and his cassock failed to hide the fact that he had a large, fat stomach. Dr. Forêt was very tall and solidly built. His long black beard was streaked with silver. During the last three decades of the nineteenth century, most of the people in L'Assomption County, whether they were country folk or townsfolk, passed through the hands of Notary Le Mire, Dr. Forêt, and the Abbé Dorval.

My parents sometimes attended weddings or funerals. They would set off in the carriage with Sambo to drive them. When they got to the house, whether it was a wedding or a funeral, the meal was usually much the same in either case. The chief difference was in the clothes worn by the guests, but, whether a young bride in white or a widow in black sat at the head of the table, the main meal was always the main meal, which meant that there was plenty to eat and that it took some time to eat it.

If the wedding breakfast was sometimes saddened by the bride's tears, funeral banquets were just as often made cheerful by the air of satisfaction of a family that had come into money or had at last got rid of a tiresome relative.

People quite often came to the manor-house on long visits. Uncles and cousins and aunts would suddenly turn up and stay for days or weeks at a time. My parents never invited people specially, but they always made their guests feel entirely welcome.

My two Salaberry aunts used to come up together from Montreal. They were my mother's sisters and a good twenty years younger than she was, for they were the children of my grandfather's second marriage. They were attractive, well-dressed girls and very fond of society. They always looked as if they had just stepped out of a Montreal drawing-room. As they brought something of the atmosphere of the big city with them, they always cheered Mother. I was particularly fond of my Aunt Thérèse, who was my godmother and who always made a fuss over me. She was an extremely pretty girl, always dressed in the height of fashion, which meant that she wore leg-of-mutton sleeves, a skirt with gathered flounces, sometimes a short bolero jacket, and, inevitably high button-boots and a little hat trimmed with flowers or a bunch of grapes.

Grand-aunt Salaberry used to come at regular intervals too. She was the colonel's third wife and thus my mother's second stepmother. She had been a Baby de Rainville before her marriage and was related to both my parents. Being a cousin as well as a stepmother, the old lady felt herself very closely linked to us and very much a member of the family.

She usually turned up during the winter. My father would have a horse hitched up to the *berlot* so that he could go and fetch her himself at the station. The *berlot* came in handy for the baggage, for Madame de Salaberry always had plenty. In addition to all her suitcases, she always brought a large number of parcels full of presents, which she distributed as soon as she arrived. There was something for everybody in the house: perfume and handkerchiefs for Mother, cigars for my father, toys for Hervé and me, and books and candies from Joyce's for my older brothers and sisters. There were presents for the servants too.

During her stay, my grandmother often went out to the kitchen to confer with Big Sophronie, who gave her recipes for especially complicated dishes. Madame de Salaberry, who kept house for her brother in Montreal, found the advice of an expert like Sophronie very useful indeed.

After she had been with us a few days, back she would go again to her duties as the mistress of a household, her receptions, her dinner-parties for twenty guests at a sitting, and her servant problems. Her brother, who had been Minister of Justice at one time, was married to an enormous woman who was very rich and who never stirred a hand about the house. My Grandmother Salaberry had to look after everything.

She was a little bit of a woman, very bright and lively, and she never seemed to be any particular age, or even to get any older. Though she was over eighty when she died, she was still just as spry and looked the same as she always had. When she married the colonel he was already nearly sixty and he died only a few months after the wedding. That was in 1882, and she left the manor-house at L'Assomption, where her elderly husband had died, to go and live with her brother, who was a judge in Montreal.

Judge Baby, as he was called, had married a Berthelet, the daughter of a former bourgeois in the North West Company. The judge some-times accompanied my grandmother when she came to the manor-house on one of her visits. He was a little man with side-whiskers and a stammer who always wore a top-hat and frock-coat. He walked with the aid of a crutch, which he held under his left armpit, and he was always nosing about all over the house. You could hear the tap-tapping of his crutch along the passages and up and down the stairs. He was an enthusiastic antiquarian and was always on the lookout for old letters or souvenirs of one sort or another. My father kept a watchful and suspicious eye on him, claiming that he was quite capable of walking off with things that didn't belong to him for the sake of adding to his collection. In the desk in the drawing-room were the three large folders full of family papers, genealogies, and officers' commissions dating from the French Régime. Whenever he heard the judge was coming on a visit, my father would exclaim, "I'm going to lock the desk with the papers; Baby would never be able to resist the temptation." As a matter of fact, when he died, the worthy judge left behind a splendid collection of manuscripts, which is known as the Baby Collection and is housed in the Sulpician Library in Montreal. Presumably not all the families he visited kept their writing-desks as carefully locked as we did ours!

Another Salaberry relation, whom we called Cousin Hermine, also used to come and stay with us for a few days at a time. She was a first cousin of my mother's, since both their fathers were sons of the famous colonel who beat the Americans at the Battle of Chateauguay in 1813. Both their fathers were also colonels. The Irumberry de Salaberrys seem to have run to colonels as other families run to lawyers or grocers, for my mother's brother was a colonel too, just like his father, his uncle, and his grandfather. Some families seem unable to escape from a persistent fate.

Cousin Hermine was a tall woman with very large feet and hands, but she was quite good-looking. She spent her whole life travelling in Europe and was always on the go between France and England and Italy, living now in Paris, now in London, now in Rome, and knowing in all three places as many people as she did in Montreal or Quebec. She became a friend of Princess Louise, later Duchess of Argyll, when this younger daughter of Queen Victoria lived in Canada as the wife of the Governor General, the Marquis of Lorne. During one of her stays in London, Cousin Hermine was presented by the Princess to the Queen at a private audience in Buckingham Palace. Cousin Hermine was always very willing to describe her presentation and it was a story that amused me intensely. The Queen had sat on a pink plush sofa in the middle of a big blue drawing-room. She wore a white widow's cap, a plain black dress, and cotton stockings. Her rather stubby arms were folded across her stomach. The Princess walked beside Cousin Hermine as far as the middle of the room and then left her to go and stand beside her royal mother. Under the scrutiny of the old Queen, Cousin Hermine advanced and made her three court curtsies. Because she was speaking to a French Canadian, the Queen had addressed her in French and, out of politeness, kept up the whole conversation in that language. I don't remember now what was said on that occasion. What intrigued me most in the whole story was the protocol at the conclusion of the audience. Cousin Hermine had to leave the room backwards, making all the proper curtsies, but without getting entangled in her long dress or in her train. Every time I heard her tell the story I waited breathlessly for the moment when she would get her feet caught in her train and fall flat on her behind in the presence of the Queen-Empress. But Hermine never did fall and, during the twenty years I remember hearing the story told, she always managed her exit without mishap.

Cousin Hermine kept on travelling until she was over seventy. She would stay for a while in Italy, go to England to visit Princess Louise, remain for a time in France with the Salaberrys at the Château de Fossé, or stay with the Gargans at Versailles. Then she would suddenly come back to Canada and turn up at the manor-house for a few days. In Montreal she lived in a boarding house and saved up money for a year or two before going off to Europe again. Sometimes Mother would say, "Hermine has forgotten us, or perhaps she's dead." But Cousin Hermine wasn't dead and she always came back, her suitcases covered with European hotel labels. I would sit and listen as she talked about Venice or Paris or London. She had seen the Pope in the Vatican, the President of the Republic at Longchamps, Queen Victoria at Balmoral. All these names of people and places fascinated me. I was longing to go off and travel as she did, to cross the ocean and see these wonderful cities and countries and own a suitcase plastered with exotic labels.

Cousin Hermine could not guess that the small boy who listened to her travel stories would one day accompany her to her last resting place.

She died when she was on one of her visits to France. By that time I had been living in Paris for some years. One day I got a letter from her saying that she was ill in Nice. By the time she reached Paris she was in critical condition and died soon afterwards in a hospital run by nuns on the Left Bank. I rode in the motor-hearse which took her remains to the Château de Fossé. Our French cousins had offered to inter the body of their Canadian kinswoman in their family vault. The funeral took place in the little church at Fossé, which is a village on the highway between Blois and Vendôme. I, her closest relative, was surrounded by our distant French cousins, the Count de Salaberry, the Count and Countess de Montlivault, Madame de Gargan, Captain du Châtelet, and the Marquis de Tristan. Together we followed her coffin, borne on the shoulders of the villagers, from the church to the cemetery, and saw Cousin Hermine off on her last journey.

As my father was an only child, our relatives on his side of the family were all rather distantly related. From time to time an old gentleman used to come and stay with us for a few days. He was

Hertel de Rouville, my father's uncle. He was a silent man who smoked incessantly and went for solitary strolls along the garden paths. Uncle Rouville lived in the province of Ontario and this was the cause of his melancholy. He himself had remained completely French, but his family up there was just as completely English; indeed none of his sons or daughters spoke a word of anything but English. Following the old French-Canadian custom, he had given his sons family names associated with the Hertels; one of them was called Fresnière, another La Broquerie. They had turned these into Frank and Brock, which didn't sound much like the old French names they had originally been given.

One fine day Uncle Rouville went off to live in Montreal. He moved into an apartment on Bleury Street and spent his days reading and smoking his pipe in a room hung with the Hertel family portraits. My father was very fond of him and used to go and see him and take me along with him. The old man hardly ever said a word. He just sat there puffing away at his pipe. As soon as we got to the door on our way out, he would take up his book and start reading again.

With nothing to do but read and smoke, he lived to quite a ripe old age. When at last he died, we went to the funeral. Uncle Rouville was laid out on a sofa in his living-room, with a taper on either side of him, dressed up in evening clothes as if he were going to a ball. From their frames along the wall his Hertel ancestors looked down on him. His English-speaking sons and daughters were all there too, lined up beside the coffin.

Uncle Rouville, lying there on his sofa, between his French ancestors and his English descendants, with his eyes closed, though all dressed up to go to a party, seemed to be reflecting on the strangeness of his situation.

Like a good many other French-Canadian families, we had a number of English-speaking relatives. After all, when two people with human impulses live side by side in the same country, there is bound to be some intermarriage between them in spite of all the differences of religion and language.

From time to time we were visited by three English-Canadian cousins called Hatt. Thomas Hatt and Patrick Hatt were on the plain side, but the remaining Hatt cousin was a fine-looking fellow. My father nicknamed them "Tomate," "Patate," and "Magnificat." We thought this very funny. Magnificent Hatt, or Magnificat, mixed

French and English words together in an amazing jumble, but Tom Hatt and Pat Hatt spoke French quite well.

Cousin Glen was another of our English-Canadian relatives. He was a doctor who lived at Chambly. As he was quite well off and had never married, my father would sometimes say jokingly that one day we would all come into a legacy from Cousin Glen, but nobody really believed it, and Cousin Glen's legacy was used as a sort of synonym for anything wildly improbable. Whenever one of us wanted to refer to something that couldn't possibly happen, they would say, "It's like Cousin Glen's legacy." Nevertheless, one fine day, we did come into a legacy from Cousin Glen. He died intestate, and so my parents and all his other cousins divided the money between them. As a matter of fact, there were a good many English-Canadian cousins, so our share only came to a few thousand dollars, but the family saying changed its meaning, and henceforth when anybody said, "It's like Cousin Glen's legacy," it meant something that, however unlikely to happen, actually had happened.

Cousin Annie was English only on her mother's side, but in her general appearance, her complexion, and the way she walked, she seemed completely English. She had been married twice and had had a number of children and all sorts of misfortunes, and yet she was still essentially very girlish and unspoilt. She often came to see us at the manor-house. Mother was very fond of her and very sorry for her too. She led a queer, unhappy sort of life and was surrounded by a vague aura of mystery and adventure. Mother, with her romantic imagination, loved to listen to Annie talk about all she did in Montreal, though there was always a certain reticence and lack of candour about her stories. She would start saying something of a confidential nature only to break off abruptly. There was always some incident or other she felt she couldn't reveal and which she took obvious pains to hide. Above all, she never "mentioned names." This constant note of suspense only served to stimulate curiosity all the more. Mother, who had spent all her life out in the country, and who had never loved anybody but her husband and her children, was greatly intrigued by a person like Annie and was always making fresh discoveries about her. Her cousin's fleeting visits gave her a sort of insight into a world where women seemed reckless and men behaved rather strangely. It was a world where, for instance, people played cards for money, where wives were not particularly interested in their husbands or their children, a world in whose drawing-rooms people spoke and acted rather like the characters in Act Two of some French play. Mother really didn't know very much about the theatre, but occasionally my father took her to Montreal to see Sarah Bernhardt or Réjane when they came on tour. Consequently, in her imagination, the domestic dramas of Montreal society were played out against a background rather like a stage setting, and she gave to the women involved the features of the actresses she had seen.

Annie looked and behaved like an innocent young girl; only the expression in her eyes showed she was a woman who had led a very chequered existence. She brought an exotic whiff of adventure into our humdrum household, and it was through her that a virtuous and utterly devoted wife and mother was able to get to know something about the lives of women of a different kind. Only because of Annie did Mother become aware that outside her own circle were others where people lived very strange lives indeed and knew no moral restraint. Whenever she heard about anyone being involved in some tangle of passion or jealousy, she would heave a sigh and say, "I expect Annie knows those people."

Cousin Annie lived to a ripe age and became a very pious old lady actively interested in all sorts of charitable organizations. She went to live as a paying guest in a convent in Montreal, and Mother used to go and visit her there. Annie no longer told half-evasive stories full of sly allusions to persons prominent in Montreal society. She had stopped seeing all her old friends and consorted entirely with nuns and the deserving poor. Only very occasionally, when Mother happened to mention a name which recalled a person or an episode out of the past would Annie give a fleeting smile, while just the suspicion of a blush coloured her pale cheeks.

One day my father received a letter which threw us all into a state of wild excitement. Monseigneur Taché was going to come and stay for a short visit. He was the Bishop of the Northwest Territories. That struck us as an amazing thing to be. The Northwest Territories was a magic phrase to us, rather like the *pays d'en haut* of which the old fur-traders used to talk. My father often told us stories of this mysterious Northwest, which his great-grand-uncle Gauthier de La Vérendrye had been the first to explore in 1740. We had heard all about Monseigneur Taché, who went out to Manitoba as a young priest and had stayed on to become first bishop of the diocese. There were still Indian tribes up there, and out on the prairies the Sioux still hunted buffalo. I had a vague idea that the bishop would come by dog-sled, wearing a bonnet of eagles' feathers in place of his mitre.

Two horses were harnessed to the "rockway" which drove off to Montreal to fetch the bishop. My father was very proud of his horses and liked to make them show their paces. Monseigneur Taché, after making one or two complimentary remarks about them, leaned over and said, "You have always had superb horses. . . . I am not feeling very well; please don't drive quite so fast."

He alighted at the manor-house porch. Everybody was out in the garden to welcome him. Mother held me by the hand, with Roque-brune, René, and Hervé on our right and my sisters on our left. The two Sophronies, Godefroy, and Sambo were with us too. As the bishop came over towards us, the June breeze stirred in the trees and the branches swayed like palm-fronds waved to greet him. A scent of roses hung in the air. The prelate gave Mother his hand and she, bending her head slightly, kissed his episcopal ring.

This was a great surprise to me and made a considerable impression at the time. I watched as my brothers and sisters and Sophronie and Sambo followed suit. They all kissed the bishop's ring in turn, but the fact that Mother had done so too made me realize what an exalted personage our visitor must be.

He spent the evening with us, and I have a hazy recollection of him sitting huddled in one of the easy-chairs in the drawing-room. He took me on his knee and stroked my hair as he talked. I couldn't keep my eyes off the stone in his ring, which gleamed as he moved his hand. My father and the bishop were quite closely related, and they were soon talking of the days when they used to meet at their Uncle Boucher de La Broquerie's in the manor-house of Sabrevois, at Boucherville, over on the other side of the St. Lawrence. Uncle Broquerie spent all his life in that old house which dated back to the seventeenth century. When he died, in 1880, he left his modest fortune to his nephews, and Monseigneur Taché wanted my father to take over the manor-house, where, according to tradition, Father de Brébeuf once stayed for some time as the guest of Pierre Boucher. However, as my parents already had the manor-house they had inherited from the seigneuresse, they didn't want to move to Boucherville.

I must have dozed off sitting in the bishop's lap, and I suppose they carried me off to bed, because I have no recollection of how the evening ended. When I woke up next morning, they told me that Monseigneur Taché had left very early with my father to drive to

Montreal. Only a few months later we got the news that the bishop had died on his return to the Northwest Territories.

I have seen photographs of Monseigneur Taché since, but they have never seemed to me to look very much like the bishop who came to see us on that June afternoon and whom we gathered in the garden to welcome. I remember him as a rather vague figure draped in a cassock with crimson buttons. I have always thought of him when reading Canadian history every time I come across the name of some old missionary or of some old Canadian bishop. These venerable figures of the past have always been typified for me by the indistinct silhouette and the flashing ring of Monseigneur Taché.

Sometimes all these visitors who came to our house when I was a child people my dreams. I see them as they were when they were alive. They wander like shadows through the corridors of my memory—shadows of another age and another world.

Big Sophronie sometimes went on shopping expeditions to the general store in the village. Some errands simply could not be confided to my mother, or to my brother Roquebrune, or to Sambo the Negro, as all were inclined to be a trifle irresponsible and forgetful. Sophronie pretended to treat these three with a sort of affectionate contempt, though, as a matter of fact, they were the three persons she was fondest of in the whole world. She had known my mother ever since the latter had come to live at the manor-house while still a little girl, and she had been devoted to her ever since. She was present when Roquebrune was born and, as he was the eldest of the boys, he was the first of my mother's children she grew to love. She saw us all come into the world, but none of the subsequent births ever seemed quite so important as that first one. As for Sambo, it was she who welcomed him in out of the cold and the snow, and this fact accounted for her attachment to him. But Sophronie never allowed her affections to blind her to people's shortcomings when it came to running errands.

She would set off with Godefroy in the carriage but usually came back on foot. There was a sort of hidden poet in Sophronie, and she liked walking home by herself along the tree-shaded road by the river.

She could take her time on the way home and saunter along as she wished. Sometimes she recited her rosary. Sophronie was very devout and often complained that she had so much work to do that she hadn't time to say her prayers, but then she used also to claim that

"Work was a form of prayer" and sometimes refused to go to Mass on Sundays because she was too busy. When my mother mentioned the matter, she would say, "The good Lord knows perfectly well that I haven't time to go to Mass today."

One day, when she had given her parcels to Godefroy, and had walked back from the village, she remarked as she came into the kitchen, "I met St. Joseph."

Sophronie said it in the same matter-of-fact way in which she might have said, "I met Dr. Forêt" or "I spoke to Monsieur Joseph-Edouard Faribault."

Nevertheless, this extraordinary statement quite confounded Little Sophronie and Sambo, who were in the kitchen at the time. So Sophronie repeated that she had just met St. Joseph.

My mother, who was well acquainted with the old servant's vivid imagination, was rather annoyed, however, when the servants told her what had been said. She tried to reason with Sophronie, but the latter stuck to her statement: she had seen St. Joseph in a vision. Nothing would budge her. As far as she was concerned, it was the most natural thing in the world.

My mother tried to get around the difficulty with a form of words.

"Look, Sophronie, you *thought* you saw St. Joseph."

"I did see him, Madame. I saw him with my own eyes."

"Yes, you did see him perhaps, but with the eyes of faith. . . . You were saying your rosary at the time, weren't you?"

"No, as a matter of fact I wasn't. I wasn't thinking about prayers at all. I was going over that recipe for stuffed veal and creamed carrots that Mademoiselle Le Prohon gave me, and. . . ."

"Now look here, Sophronie, you aren't going to stand there and tell me that while you were thinking of your stuffed veal St. Joseph chose that precise moment to appear to you."

"Well, that's just the way it was, Madame. I looked up and there was St. Joseph, right in front of me on the road."

"And just what did St. Joseph look like?" asked my mother in a sceptical tone of voice.

"Why, he . . . he looked like St. Joseph. What a funny question! Madame knows quite well what St. Joseph looks like. He had his staff with a flower at the end of it and his pink robe and his little beard."

So saying Sophronie looked her mistress up and down with a pitying expression.

My mother couldn't really bring herself to believe that St. Joseph was in the habit of going for walks along the highway and of making sudden appearances to the people he happened to meet, so she spoke to the Abbé Dorval about Sophronie's vision. The good priest was very much embarrassed by this strange business.

He was almost inclined to believe the story at first but, being Sophronie's confessor, he was a bit leery of her somewhat unstable imagination. "The saints do queer things sometimes," he said. "They've been known to appear to people who weren't at all worthy of such an honour. And people who see visions aren't always sainted persons themselves either. It's hard to tell. Maybe St. Joseph wants us to build him a shrine on the highway from Montreal to L'Assomption."

Sophronie, for her part, stopped talking about St. Joseph and seemed to have forgotten the whole incident. Still, she never would say she hadn't had the vision. As far as she was concerned, she had seen St. Joseph with her own eyes, and sometimes she would say in a perfectly matter-of-fact way: "That was the same month I saw St. Joseph" or "that time St. Joseph appeared to me."

However, Sophronie wasn't the sort of woman to make a fuss about her vision or to cause people any trouble, and St. Joseph made a great mistake if he was counting on her to enhance his prestige. She had absolutely no desire to play the part of a visionary or to make people talk about herself and St. Joseph. But the saint had appeared to her; she insisted there could be no possible doubt about it, and that's all there was to it. In any case, it was a private matter between her and St. Joseph and didn't really concern anybody else.

No one ever did manage to get to the bottom of Big Sophronie's story about her vision. Was she the victim of a delusion that day when she thought she saw St. Joseph coming towards her along the river road, or did the saint really manifest his presence to gladden her poor old heart?

Perhaps a miracle did actually occur. If it did, it led to nothing, because it was a great mistake to suppose that Sophronie was the sort of person who would take on an advertising campaign to whip up the ardour of the saint's devotees.

Many things happen that leave no trace behind them. No one can hope to keep track of all the inconsequential days and hours in a lifetime.

Moreover, it's easier to remember what others did than what one did oneself. Most children are very observant and notice with great interest everything that happens around them even though they are hardly conscious of their own existence. A man of sixty will often succeed in retracing his steps back to that forgotten period of his life. He will find it is all still there, clearly etched in his memory like some changeless landscape. There is the house, standing in the middle of the garden. There are the flowers in all their natural colours, and the dogs still barking. The door to the dining-room stands open; the table is laid. Mother is sitting at one end of it and Sambo comes in from the kitchen with the blue china soup-tureen clutched between his two black hands. The whole family is gathered around the table and there is a scraping of chairs as they take their places. They are all sitting where they usually sit: my father, Roquebrune, René, Hervé, and my sisters. Their voices are the same as they always were and their expressions as lively as ever. In that vast, low-ceilinged room with its polished beams none of the furniture has been changed; the same pictures hang on the wall and the silver teapot, standing on the dark mahogany sideboard, reflects the light from one of the windows.

There is only one person missing: I myself.

The process of remembering consists in recalling the external world as it was, in recreating places that have vanished, in bringing back from the dead an entire family. The only one of them all who is still alive is precisely the one who seems most elusive, and that is one's own self. It is impossible for a person to see himself in such a setting.

It is our senses that lead us to our knowledge of people and of things and to our mastery of the external world which they constitute. Those faces that I got to know so well, those familiar objects that I came in contact with each day, the smell of flowers, tables and chairs and pictures, the animals of the household, and all its sounds, made their impression on my child's brain, which before had been a blank, and this impression remains, intact, precise, and alive, though the child that I was no longer exists. It is just as if my parents and my brothers and sisters, our house, and all the things that formed my surroundings in those days still exist and I alone am dead and gone.

I remember with special vividness the events of one particular day in my childhood. Perhaps it is because on that occasion I experienced

D

a set of completely new and intense emotions for the very first time. I might well have forgotten that day, as I have forgotten so many others, but it is all there still with its background of deep blue sky and a white expanse of snow against which the trees stand out with their trunks and branches black and bare. It was a very cold day; the road was sheathed with ice and the horses' hooves rang out against it. There was a music of sleigh-bells and the creak and jingle of harness. Up in the front part of the *berlot* stood Godefroy, muffled up to his ears and shouting, "Whoa! Back up!"

Every winter, in January, when it became really cold, Godefroy set aside several days for ice-cutting. It was a difficult job and he was the only one with sufficient experience to undertake it. He had to fill the ice-house behind the shed with great blocks of ice, covered with sawdust, which would last without melting away until the following September. This ice-house was built half underground, and Big Sophronie would go there in the hot weather to fetch ice to put around the meat lying on the shelves in the pantry.

All this ice came from the river. The little stream that ran close by the house froze hard, just like most of the other lakes and rivers and streams in Canada, but for some unknown reason we didn't get our ice from there. We got it from the St. Lawrence itself, out in front of St. Sulpice, for that is the spot where Godefroy used to cut it. He had picked this place as a man might pick out a particular corner of his garden for his choicest fruit. He always drove home with a shining load of blue-green blocks. When the *berlot* with its team of horses turned into the avenue leading to the manor-house, Godefroy seemed to be driving a fairy-chariot loaded with materials for building a translucent palace.

Jacques used to lend Godefroy a hand, and my brothers always went along too. Sambo was excluded from these expeditions because he hated very cold weather and couldn't face the idea of venturing right out on the surface of the river where it flowed past in front of the wharf at St. Sulpice. It was my dearest ambition to be allowed to go along with them, but Mother had never let me go, as she was afraid the long, cold trip would be too much for me. But when, on one occasion, Hervé came back and told me everything they had done, I was keener still to go along with the ice-cutters. Mother finally decided to let me go.

As extra protection on an expedition of this sort, a fuzzy, red, woollen scarf, called a "cloud," was added to my usual outdoor winter clothing. It was wound around my neck and I could use it to protect my face if I needed to. In all other respects I was dressed just like my brothers or Jacques or Godefroy; that is to say, I had a big, thick, grey overcoat and a red tuque such as all French Canadians wore in winter in those days. Around my waist was an arrow-patterned sash, and I wore moccasins too because we intended to go snow-shoeing while the men did their ice-cutting.

It was very cold and dry and there wasn't a breath of wind. I was huddled up with my brothers on the floor of the *berlot* under the bear-skins that were used for sleigh-rugs, and it was as if we were in a little house on runners. The cold was all around us but we were protected from it. Godefroy, sitting up in front, wasn't quite so fortunate. The driving-seat of a Canadian *berlot* was just a leather strap strung between two uprights. It made an odd sort of seat but Godefroy seemed quite at home on it. The back seat had been taken out to make room for the blocks of ice, and that is why we had been able to set up our shelter. Whenever I ventured to look out, I could see the driver's grey back, his red woollen tuque, and the horses' rumps tossing and jingling the bells with which their harness was hung.

Nowhere in the world has the light such a special quality as it has in Canada during the winter. The first houses of St. Sulpice seemed almost within reach though they were still really quite a long way off. I felt as if I could stretch out my hand and almost touch the farm-houses, the great, bare trees lost in a waste of snow, the big wooden barns looking like the pictures of Noah's Ark in Sambo's Bible. The air was so clear that everything stood out in the sharpest possible relief from the white background.

The runners of the sleigh made a high, screeching sound that seemed to me like the voice of winter itself, the voice of the cold. I have often heard that sound since on the icebound roads of the province of Quebec. The screeching of the runners and the music of the sleigh-bells were familiar to me all through my childhood and composed a symphony of silvery, staccato sounds that I always associate with that sunny day when the snow was so dazzlingly white and I was so happy.

Godefroy drove the *berlot* right out on to the river before reining in the horses, and then we jumped out on the ice. There was a big, shining patch clear of snow right in front of the wharf at St. Sulpice, but out beyond there were drifts of snow. Because of the wind, sections of the frozen river were swept clear and others around them were banked high with snow. Once we had our snow-shoes on, we could go clear across the frozen surface to the villages on the other shore, and that is just what my brothers intended to do. However, before we could start out, Jacques had to go and take the horses to the stable over at the Lantiers' place.

The Lantiers were friends of ours and they lived in a house beside the road not far from the wharf. It was a big wooden house, and I had been there before in summer with my parents. We were all sure of a hearty welcome.

Once the horses were unharnessed, Jacques led them off by their bridles up the steep, slippery slope, and we accompanied him. Godefroy stayed behind on the ice and started in with his pick-axe.

The door was opened by kind-hearted Madame Lantier herself, and she was soon surrounded by a noisy throng. She quickly undid my scarf and sash and took off my heavy coat and tuque. We found ourselves in the big living-room, where the table was laid, as it always seemed to be when I was there. The Lantiers gave the general impression of expecting guests for a never-ending succession of meals. This big room was their drawing-room, dining-room and kitchen all in one. They had knocked down the partitions of several rooms to make one big, convivial centre, and there they managed to live a life of cheerful plenty. At one end was the stove and a big table surrounded by all the pots and pans; this was the kitchen. The middle part was the dining-room, which consisted of two big sideboards, chairs and a table with leaves. The rest of the room was the drawing-room with its horsehair sofas, its easy-chairs and its what-nots. A staircase led up from the middle of the room to the upper storey where the bedrooms were.

Monsieur Lantier made his appearance at this stage, walking carefully down the staircase. He was a big, rheumatic man with a pink complexion and a hearty, jovial manner. This hospitable couple had three sons and a daughter. All the Lantier boys were very tall, and Eveline, the daughter, looked almost slight by comparison. I thought she was very beautiful.

The three sons were interested in live-stock and each of them specialized in one aspect of the work. The eldest one looked after the cows and made the butter and cheese, which he sold at Bon-Secours Market in Montreal. The youngest one had charge of the bulls, the oxen and the young calves. The remaining son supervised the pigpens. Eveline had a share in the farm-work too, and her job was to look after the chickens. This hard-working family believed in good food and plenty of it. They were always serving up enormous meals and there was inevitably a stew-pot bubbling away on the stove in the big living-room. Succulent odours of meats and gravies permeated the whole room. Madame Lantier herself was a very fine cook; even our own Big Sophronie had a high regard for her and admitted that she was absolutely first class.

Obviously we were expected to have dinner before doing anything else. In Canada, the midday meal was called dinner and the evening meal supper. Madame Lantier didn't even bother to ask us to join them; that was taken for granted. All they had to do was to add a few leaves to the table. The three Lantier boys came in from the stables and the pigpen to greet us with great shouts and roars of laughter. I was caught up in the air to be hugged and kissed.

From the living-room windows you could look out on four different scenes. In front was the ice-bound river with its snow-drifts and, far off in the distance, the south shore, which you could hardly make out, even on a clear day. Behind were the farmyard and the sheds and the stables and the chicken-run, while on either side stood big houses rather like the Lantiers' with gabled roofs and wooden verandas. In the old settlements in the province of Quebec, particularly in the ones along the river, the "concessions," which date back to Louis XIV's day, are all very long and narrow. That is why the houses are fairly close to one another. It meant that people could lend each other a hand if the Indians attacked. Most of these properties have kept their original boundaries and run back in long, narrow strips to the woods.

I looked out from the back window and saw Jacques coming in from the stable. There was a girl beside him, walking in step with him. They seemed very absorbed in one another and stopped on the steps for quite a time before coming into the house. Eveline looked up at the young man with a smile. I could see their faces, glowing with cold, and the movement of their lips through the frost-covered panes. I tapped on the window and they turned around suddenly and saw me standing there.

A gust of cold air swept into the living-room as they opened the door. I ran over and threw myself into Eveline's arms. I always liked to stroke her rosy cheeks, all fresh and cold from the outdoors. She carried me over towards the stove, slipping the shawl from her head. She kept it about her shoulders though, and its long folds hung down and covered her workaday dress. In those days, women and girls in the country districts always wore shawls in the wintertime. These were part of their regular costume and protected them against the cold when they went out to the stables or the hen-house.

Eveline dumped me down in an easy-chair beside the big stove and tripped upstairs to disappear into her bedroom. She came down a few minutes later wearing a pretty blue dress, and she had had time to do her hair too. We all stared at her as she came downstairs and I noticed that she was blushing.

This staircase, rising from the centre of the big living-room, was a special feature of the Lantier house. Anybody who went up or down it couldn't help being seen by everybody else in the room. I think that was the first time I noticed how pretty Eveline was. She was all smiles, and it was quite obvious that she was delighted by our visit, though as a matter of fact, she usually was smiling and was one of those persons who always manage to look happy and cheerful. When she reached the bottom step, Eveline stopped and looked about as if somebody were missing from the room. I got the impression that her smile was on the point of fading from her lips. She seemed worried about something, so I rushed over to her, grabbed her by both hands and pulled her down from the staircase. As I hung round her neck, I put my face close to hers and whispered in her ear, "Dinner's ready and so Jacques has gone to fetch Godefroy; he'll be back in a minute." I was delighted to see this adorable girl's face light up again with a smile.

Dinner was one of those traditional Lantier affairs; which is to say, that there was lots of talk and laughter and plenty of good things to eat. I looked forward especially to dessert because I had seen Madame Lantier making a huge caramel custard crowned with meringue, but before we got to that stage we had to wade through pea soup, roast pork with vegetables and then cheese. Monsieur Lantier sat at one end of the table with my brothers René and Hervé at his right and left, while Roquebrune and I sat on either side of Madame Lantier. Godefroy had taken his place between two of the sons of the house, and Jacques was next to Eveline. She had to get up every now and then to go and fetch the next course from the kitchen or to change the plates. That was my signal to run out and help. In this way I had the privilege of carrying in the wonderful dessert myself and of putting it down in front of the mistress of the house.

In spite of being so busy waiting at table, I caught snatches of the conversation between Godefroy and the Lantier boys and learned that they were all going to get together on the ice-cutting right after dinner. I also found out that my brother and I were to go on a snow-shoeing expedition to the south shore with Jacques and Eveline.

The Lantiers couldn't exactly be described as habitants. In those days in Canada, though society was relatively democratic, there were subtle gradations which separated people and families and professional groups from one another into distinct layers.

As Jacques was a habitant's son, he was rather inclined to look up to the Lantiers. These stock-breeders were well-to-do and they had tradespeople and a notary among their relatives. On Madame Lantier's side there was a bishop and several priests. All this made them seem pretty important people to the young man, so his affection for Eveline was heightened by a touch of self-esteem.

She, for her part, loved Jacques with the utter and passionate un-selfishness of a really generous woman, though her feelings were not unmixed with anxiety. Could she really count on marrying him some day?

To live in a village in the province of Quebec in those days was rather like living in a goldfish bowl, quite cut off from the outside world. The most trifling event in any family remained a topic of conversation among all their friends and acquaintances for months. I was constantly hearing people talking about legacies and marriages and engagements. Big Sophronie had always been quite sure that Jacques and Eveline would make a match of it, but not everybody in the manor-house, or even in the kitchen, was of the same opinion. Godefroy didn't think Jacques wanted to get married and, one day when they were all discussing the question, he introduced a new angle. "I think," he said, "that Jacques wants to be a priest."

I was amazed at this. Jacques a priest! Like the Abbé Dorval with white hair and a fat stomach? I just couldn't imagine Jacques wearing a cassock and a shovel hat. I preferred to go on thinking that he and Eveline would get married. There would be a big dinner at the Lantiers'; we would all be asked to it, and have lots and lots to eat. Then Jacques and Eveline would go and live in a clapboard house with a veranda around it. There would be a garden and dogs and cats and I would go and visit them as often as I could. I thought people's lives were arranged just as simply as that, and that there was always a happy ending to everything.

After a dinner like the one we had just eaten, the cold out-of-doors didn't bother us in the least. French Canadians have always had two ways of overcoming the cold: they have huge stoves stoked to the brim with wood or coal in their houses and huge meals tucked away inside their stomachs. After a dinner consisting of pork, potatoes, cheese, scalding hot tea, cakes, cream and maple syrup, a person can face the severest cold with equanimity. I had to take my mittens off to tie the leather thongs of my snow-shoes. My face and hands were bare, but even with no protection from the cold, I couldn't feel anything at all, except a gentle warmth coursing through my limbs. As far as I was concerned, the cold just didn't exist, and certainly it had no effect on me. The frozen river, with its vast expanse of snow and ice, was just a great empty space for us to run about on with our snow-shoes.

When I was a youngster, snow-shoes had not yet been replaced by skis. Snow-shoeing was the great winter sport. You wore moccasins and fixed the snow-shoes to them with leather thongs. Then you could walk on the snow without sinking in. In the old days, that is from the days of Louis XIII of France to those of Victoria of England, French Canadians travelled, traded for furs and fought their battles on snow-shoes. It was with snow-shoes on their feet that the *coureurs des bois* went to buy beaver skins in the villages of the Hurons or the Iroquois, returning with great packs on their backs which they sold to the traders in Quebec or Montreal. It was on snow-shoes that Gauthier de La Vérendrye and his sons explored all the North West, where no white man had been before, that Le Moyne d'Iberville and his brothers, Maricourt and Sainte-Hélène, seized the English forts on Hudson's Bay, and that François de Hertel, in 1690, at the head of fifty men, stormed a frontier town in New England. It was on snow-shoes that the agents of the North West Company travelled from treaty fort to factory on the business of their great fur-trading concern. The Jesuit missionaries wore snow-shoes too, to cross the snowy wastes with sacks full of provisions and copies of the Gospels translated into an Indian language.

Snow-shoeing had been just a practical concern with the heroes and saints of the Colony in its glorious early days, but by the end of the nineteenth century it had degenerated into a sort of game. But it was still very popular. All little French Canadians were taught to walk on the snow by means of these wooden frames criss-crossed with cat-gut. I learned the secrets and the fine points of snow-shoeing from my brothers. René was particularly good at it.

He was the nimblest, the strongest and the most daring of the four of us. My father used to nickname him the Chevalier de La Roque after a distant great-grand-uncle who bore that name and had led a particularly adventurous life.

Seafaring was the great adventure in those days, so the Chevalier de La Roque went to sea, but he had adventures in other spheres as well. René certainly had the inclinations and the temperament of a genuine adventurer. He had a great talent for outdoor sports of all kinds. Country life had made him physically very active. He rode as if he had been born in the saddle, skated to perfection and could hold his own as a hunter with my father and Jacques. On snow-shoes he could outrace us all.

René went off like a shot with Roquebrune and Hervé following him. I had been delayed by having to adjust my snow-shoes, which was a difficult job. When at last I was ready, my brothers were already disappearing into the distance and were just black dots against the snow. I couldn't hope to catch up with them; they had got too far ahead of me. Anyway I knew René had left me behind on purpose, as my presence annoyed him. With my short, stubby legs, I couldn't keep up with my brothers' swift stride. That meant they had to stop and help me over the rough places, which slowed them down. What René really liked to do was to dash off at full speed and cover a lot of ground so that when he got back he could say they had gone for miles. I was just a very small boy and couldn't hope to keep pace with them.

I was disappointed, though, and didn't know what to do. My usual playmate, the delightful Hervé, had been caught up in the excitement of the expedition and had gone off with the other two, leaving me to my own resources. It looked as if I was going to be forced to choose between a short tramp on my own or going back to the Lantiers'. It would be boring to have to sit beside the stove between Monsieur Lantier having his after-dinner nap and Madame Lantier doing her knitting. I wouldn't even have a chance of going to see the stables and the pigpens with the Lantier boys, because they had gone off to help Godefroy with the ice-cutting. I could see them now out on the river beyond the wharf. They had made a hole already and, with their cross-cut saws, were quarrying out big blocks of ice which they piled on to the sleigh. I sauntered over to watch them work but Godefroy didn't like the idea of my standing so close to the hole, so he ordered me off.

It was just at that moment that I saw Jacques and Eveline appear over the crest of the river bank. They made their way down on to the ice and started to put on their snow-shoes, so I ran over towards them.

Eveline had had to stay behind after dinner to help with the tidying up and Jacques had been chatting to Monsieur Lantier while he waited for her. Eveline was very lively and seemed bubbling over with happiness. Her face was half hidden by her fur collar and only a few curls managed to peep out from under her red tuque. She was really very pretty and Jacques smiled as he looked her up and down. Then he knelt on one knee to fasten the thongs of Eveline's snow-shoes. Kneeling there he looked rather as if he were worshipping the goddess of winter.

They were particularly nice to me and, whether or not I interfered with their plans for an excursion alone together, at least they didn't show it. They also took short steps so that I could easily keep up with them. We crossed a wide expanse of snow and then came to another stretch of ice. We had to be especially careful going over this slippery part, but at last we came to a place where the wind had piled up more snowdrifts. I managed to scramble up to the top with some difficulty. There, right in front of me, was the south shore. A church steeple and a row of houses stood out quite clearly; in fact they seemed to be close at hand, but I knew we were really still a longish way away from them.

Every now and then I turned to make some remark or other to my two companions. They seemed to be worried as to whether I was getting tired or cold, but I didn't want to stop. However, Jacques finally decided that we had come far enough, since on our way back to the north shore we would have the wind against us. I didn't argue the matter and struck out in the lead again on the way back. It had got a good deal colder. We were facing the wind now and it was very gusty and penetrating. I had to turn my back to it every now and then because my cheeks and nose were so cold. When I did so, I noticed that Jacques and Eveline were walking hand in hand.

She seemed to be moving along in a dream and I think she would have been prepared to go on across the frozen river for hours, hand in hand with Jacques, quite oblivious to either fatigue or cold.

Sleighs, often drawn by teams of horses, made a practice of crossing on the ice from one shore to the other. There was a regular highway for vehicles and pedestrians marked out by small spruce trees stuck in the snow. I headed for this temporary road. A big *berlot*, drawn at a trot by two horses abreast, was making for the north shore and loomed up larger the closer it got to us. When I could hear the jingle of the bells I waved to the habitant to show him I wanted him to stop for me. A man driving a *berlot* would never refuse this favour to anyone. "Whoa, back up there!" I took off my snow-shoes and climbed into the back seat calling out to Jacques and Eveline to join me, which they did. The habitant gave a flick of his whip and the *berlot* sped off again across the ice. It was getting dark fast and much colder too. The frozen river was just a vague, white blur as I buried myself deeper in the buffalo robes of the sleigh.

Jacques and Eveline were on either side of me and this helped to keep me warm. It was somehow oddly pleasant to feel their two bodies pressed against mine. The snow-shoeing had tired me, and now, with the motion of the sleigh, I began to feel drowsy. I leaned my head against Eveline and dozed off a little. With one arm around my shoulders she held me close against her otter-skin. For a moment I slept and dreamed, and then the cold woke me up again, quite suddenly. Jacques and Eveline seemed to be just on the point of kissing each other, though I couldn't be quite sure it wasn't all part of my dream.

Later, much later, I often thought about that kiss. Indeed the memory of that particular moment lived on in my mind and I was never to forget it altogether. I have often thought of the sleigh gliding across the ice, the wind whistling about me, the light fading over the great expanse of whiteness, and there, just a few inches from my face, two pairs of lips meeting. In that precise second a whole unknown world was revealed to me for the first time—the world of love.

I often thought of those two, long after Jacques was dead and Eveline had taken the veil as a nun, and when I did so, I didn't see them in my mind's eye as I so often had in actual reality, standing in the sunshine, laughing and full of life, but as two serious-faced young people, scarcely visible against the twilight, drawing closer to one another for the kiss.

When we got back to the Lantiers', my three brothers had already arrived. They had gone for miles on their snow-shoes and René's nose was slightly frost-bitten. Hervé had a sore left heel which, according to René, proved that he didn't really know how to snow-shoe.

Godefroy and the Lantier boys had finished their job, and the *berlot* was piled high with huge blocks of ice. Jacques was hitching up the team of horses and we were all ready to start, but before leaving Madame Lantier gave us all a cup of scalding hot coffee and a piece of cake, and when at last we left the house, and were shouting our good-byes, I discovered that my pockets had been generously stuffed with chunks of maple cream.

Godefroy had spread bear-rugs on top of the load of ice, and we climbed up on these for the ride home. When the sleigh drew up before the kitchen porch, and Big Sophronie opened the door with a lantern held out at arm's length, we must have looked, seated on our icy throne, like some of those Kings of the North she used to tell us about in her stories.

And so we came home with a whole load of glistening blocks of ice—blocks which were frozen pieces of the river.

Some men, and some women too, find it hard to come to grips with reality. From their childhood on they are unable to cope with it; even the process of growing up makes no difference to them. They seem to live out their lives in a dream-world, which stands between them and reality. That is what sometimes accounts for a certain hesitancy in their speech, a half-smile on their lips and a sleepy, far-away look in their eyes.

Hervé was quite cut off from the world in which he lived. He always seemed to be somewhere else. As a child, he rarely had anything to say for himself, and used to ask sudden, unrelated questions which showed how far away his thoughts really were. He lived in a universe of dreams and imagination. He was always busy creating his own world and peopling it with beings of his own devising, or else he was off in some private faraway land, known only to him. When he returned from one of his imaginary journeys, he always had a distant look in his eyes and hardly seemed to see ordinary objects around about him. Sometimes, on those occasions, he seemed to make a special effort to show us that he really was quite interested in us and would ask some question or other to indicate concern about some recent happening.

He shared the lessons Mademoiselle Villeneuve gave my sisters in the schoolroom. This little old lady lived in the village and came to the manor-house three times a week to pass on her knowledge to us children. At the time, I was thought to be too young to take part in

the lesson-periods, so I was always in a hurry for Hervé to finish, as
he was my regular playmate. He was three years older than I was,
and I stood very much in awe of his greater experience and wisdom,
which I thought I would never be able to emulate. Hervé used the
stories he read about in books to form a basis for our games. As I
had complete confidence in his genius, I followed out all his instructions and accepted the dramatic conventions he dictated to the letter.

The attic upstairs and the sheds behind the house were the theatres
where my brother's dramatic creations took shape. The attic was the
favourite spot of all. Under its beams and rafters, we acted out the
adventures of a thousand fabulous and fantastic characters. Coming
down from up there, in my case, always meant an immediate return
to everyday life and the world of reality, but Hervé lived on in his
private dream-world. His thoughts were often still upstairs in the
attic.

As ordinary life bored him, he transformed it to suit himself. His
mind had magic properties of its own, but he borrowed his best
creations from books. For quite a long time fairy tales were a
favourite source. To me, *Beauty and the Beast* was a game in the attic
long before I knew it as a tale by Madame de Beaumont.

So it was that, thanks to Hervé, I came to know a whole field of
literature by acting it out. I saw him dressed as Golo abducting a
Geneviève de Brabant represented by a couple of old pillows wrapped
in a silk dress full of holes and all torn at the pleats. Mother had
given it to us for our stage wardrobe. He had plenty of other properties too. The attic itself provided a great variety of usable objects, but
Hervé was sometimes as exacting as any actor-manager and would
go and ask my mother or my sisters or Sophronie to let him have
some particular article which he needed for an especially elaborate
effect. He always took the principal part himself and I was left to fill
in. He played Captain Hatteras and the children of Captain Grant
too, all by himself. I remember seeing him do Bois-Rosé and Costal
the Indian. It was my job to act the part of the devoted sailor or the
bewildered Paganel. At other times, I was the enemy being pursued
and finally overtaken and vanquished. On one particular occasion,
when I had been fastened to the stake, and was waiting to be put to
death with frightful tortures, Hervé's terrifying costume, together
with the faces he made, his threatening gestures, and the weapons he
brandished, threw me into a regular panic. I managed to tear myself
loose from my bonds and dashed downstairs howling, to throw my-

self all a-tremble into the comforting arms of Sophronie. When I saw Hervé again at dinner that evening, he refrained from scolding me, though when he looked in my direction, there was a hint of both irony and pity in his charming smile. He was the misunderstood poet in the presence of a crass materialist. I had been silly enough to think that his make-believe was real.

Shahrazad was never more inventive than my brother Hervé. The sultan's favourite had to think up a new story every evening; Hervé, the disciple and imitator of the Oriental fabulist, must have dreamed each night when he went to bed of the play he was going to act out next day under the attic roof. As a matter of fact, the *Arabian Nights* was one of his favourite sources for plots for quite a long time. With a turban made out of an old shawl around his head, and wearing a flowered dressing-gown and an arrow-patterned sash around his middle, he was Sinbad the Sailor, Aladdin and a dozen or so other characters that figure in the Galland translation. This magic book with its illustrations, a book we knew almost by heart, was kept propped open on an old chest. It was the work of reference to which we went for details of costume and setting (not that we were particularly hard to please in such matters). Neither Hervé nor I were at all literal-minded on this subject. Like Shakespeare's actors, we had traditions of our own that freed us from the ordinary conventions of stagecraft. Our imagination sufficed to fill in the odd gap here and there. As in Queen Elizabeth's day, a lantern in a corner of the stage did very well for moonlight; an old chest, at angles in just the right place, could be a wall, a prison or a window.

The attic really provided a wonderful treasure-trove of stage costumes and properties. Even children without any imagination at all would have found hundreds of things to set them dreaming. Hervé and I had plenty to stimulate our reveries, for under the rafters of the attic was a century's accumulation of furniture, clothing, and miscellaneous articles which together formed the weirdest collection imaginable. Whenever the worm-eaten legs of an easy-chair gave way and it collapsed on to the floor, or a table became too rickety for further use, it was put up in the attic. There was enough there to furnish a whole house. One huge cupboard was crammed full of dresses and overcoats, old-fashioned cloaks, frock-coats, and top-hats. Sophronie would go up and rummage around from time to time, and would throw in a few moth-balls or rescue some article of clothing that Little Sophronie, who was a skilled seamstress, could re-make into something wearable for the village poor. One could always be sure of finding what one wanted there whenever the need arose: a length of material, or an old coat for some tramp that came knocking at the kitchen door. Sometimes Sophronie would suddenly find a use for one of our more precious "properties" and take it away from us, but there was always an inexhaustible supply left.

The *catalognes* and arrow-patterned sashes were our favourite stage-properties. At that time the *catalogne* was the standard type of carpet in Canada for houses out in the country. These long, multi-coloured strips were woven by the wives of the habitants and were always found on kitchen floors. The women made them out of rags. This unique handicraft was started in the days of the Intendant, Jean Talon, who administered Canada in Louis XIV's time. The weaving of *catalognes* was actually invented by a seigneuresse, Madame Le Gardeur de Repentigny. Nobody has ever been able to find out why they were called *catalognes*. Perhaps it was a distant influence from the Spanish colonies—Mexico or Louisiana—brought back by fur-traders or *voyageurs* in Cavalier de La Salle's day, or by comrades of Louis Jolliet, who discovered the Mississippi. The floor of the kitchen in the manor-house was completely carpeted with *catalognes*. These were changed quite frequently; it went without saying that they should always look new and unfaded. Once or twice a year Godefroy gave them a thorough washing, but as soon as their colours began to go, my mother bought new ones from a woman in the village who specialized in making them. Then the old ones would be relegated to the attic.

The arrow-patterned sashes hung from nails driven into the rafters. Their dominant reds gave the huge attic the appearance of an Indian tent, and their long fringes looked like scalps, grisly trophies of some Iroquois triumph. Up until the middle of the nineteenth century, L'Assomption County was the chief centre for the manufacture of arrow-patterned sashes. The habitants' wives wove them for the factors of the North West Company, who bought them in considerable quantities. Around 1850, Manitoba and the "Territories", which is what people called the whole vast region of western Canada, was entirely dominated by the Company. At that time the fur-trade still took pride of place in Canadian commerce, and the richest families of Montreal were descended from former directors of the Company. It employed a whole army of factors, who spent their lives in the trading-posts scattered over Manitoba, the Territories, the Rocky

Mountains and the Pacific Coast. The directors, who were known as *Bourgeois*, were usually Scottish or French, Simon McTavish, Nicolas Montour, the Marquis Rastel de Rocheblave and Chaboillez are some of the best-known ones. These adventurers made huge fortunes for themselves on a grand scale. The Company had a rigid hierarchy of rank and the more important members formed a veritable aristocracy in Montreal, where their famous club was situated. To become a member of the Beaver Club, a man had to be a *Bourgeois*, a factor or an officer in the Company's service—an officer, that is, of the Company's own troops which were known as Guides. The Company was a real power in its own right and, at the time of Confederation, in 1867, the Dominion Government had to take this fact into serious consideration.

From my father's stories, Hervé and I had learned a good deal about the North West Company and fur-traders in general. One of my great-grandfather's cousins commanded the Guides in 1820. He was called André de Roquebrune and was the hero of a whole host of adventures among the Sioux, the Crees and other western Indian tribes. He had been an enormously powerful man, over six feet tall, and his courage and his physical beauty became a legend among the Indians of the West, who greatly admire these two qualities. Among the family papers in the writing-desk in the drawing-room were some very remarkable letters from André de Roquebrune, commanding officer of the Guides. In Louis XV's day, my father's great-great-grandfather, Louis La Roque de Roquebrune, travelled far and wide with his cousin, the Chevalier de Tonty, who was a celebrated fur-trader. There was also the case of my maternal grandfather, Colonel de Salaberry, who served as an officer in the Northwest, in 1865, in Riel's war against the Canadian government. When I was a boy, old Mademoiselle de Rocheblave, the Marquis' daughter, was still living in Montreal. She was very wealthy and owned one of the old houses with a veranda in the St. Louis de France district. There she entertained her guests with magnificent banquets that took four hours to serve. Once or twice a winter my parents used to go into town to have dinner with the daughter of the former *Bourgeois* of the Company. L'Assomption Village served as a trading-post for many years and, when I was a boy, a warehouse that had been used there for storing beaver pelts was still standing. Laurent Le Roux, who travelled with Mackenzie, the man who discovered the great river that bears his name on the maps of Canada, was a native of L'Assomption. I remember the house where he lived, next door to the church. He died there one day, listening peacefully to the Angelus after a long and adventurous life spent in the Territories.

For us, the arrow-patterned sashes symbolized all these heroes of the Northwest. When we handled one or other of these long strips of coloured wool, it recalled all the stories my father had told us about these men. The Company itself had long since passed out of existence, the last *Bourgeois* had been dead for half a century and maps of Canada no longer showed the Territories, but that chapter of history still lived on under the rafters of our attic. Sheltering under tents made of *catalogne* and with arrow-patterned sashes around our waists, my brother and I were La Vérendrye discovering the Rockies, McTavish trading with the Indians, André de Roquebrune at the head of his regiment of Guides, Mackenzie and Laurent Le Roux paddling down the giant river that leads to the Pole. Their names may have been forgotten and their memory largely effaced, but they lived again in the make-believe of two little boys who were fascinated by the magic of their adventures. We added this company of Canadians, whose deeds belonged to the past, to Sinbad the Sailor, Captain Hatteras and even D'Artagnan, thus mixing history and legend, the heroes of the Northwest Territories and the characters created by Shahrazad, Jules Verne and Alexandre Dumas.

Hervé's interests suddenly seemed to change. He became very religious; he was always saying his prayers and dreamed of living a consecrated life and becoming a priest. From that time forward he let me play all the best parts in our theatre up in the attic. I was the chief now, or the captain, or the emperor; he played the missionary or even the martyr, as the case might be. The *catalognes* and arrow-patterned sashes were now used as altar-cloths; he was the officiating priest, and I, a bored and rather mutinous congregation. At his entreaty, Mother agreed to give him a whole set of church "ornaments" for Christmas, and he now had the complete paraphernalia for playing at priest. His favourite reading was the *Lives of the Saints* and it was from them that he chose the subjects for our theatricals. That made for quite a change up in the attic. We now walked around and around it in procession, as if in a chapel, and the walls were decorated with holy pictures. The old skirts and frock-coats in the cupboard were cut up into cassocks for us to wear, while Hervé chanted and genuflected and conducted innumerable services. The four volumes of the

Lives of the Saints, edited by the Benedictine Fathers, usurped the place of the *Arabian Nights*; Shahrazad and Jules Verne were banned. The very same attic which had been a magic cave for the sultan's favourite, the deck of a ship in a storm, or a fur-trading post, was now a holy place sanctified by the prayers of a boy playing at saint.

Hervé developed a special veneration for St. Louis of Gonzaga, for St. Benedict Labré, for Father Brébeuf, and used to act out their lives. I took part in all these sacred dramas and was much impressed. Of course, I didn't always understand what he was driving at, and I didn't really do very well in the small parts he condescended to give me. He soon gave me up as a possible convert and restricted my acting to playing the part of the faithful congregation. So I sat on a trunk and watched him say his masses. Decked out in his cassock, and with a stole around his neck, he would advance on me with lowered eyes and offer me Communion in the form of slices of apple. Rather bewildered by all this, I would kneel down and receive the viaticum. But I soon got bored by it all and sometimes I would refuse to go up to church, that is, to climb up to the attic to listen to my brother's sermons and gulp down pieces of chopped-up apple. Hervé was very annoyed by these signs of revolt on the part of his faithful flock. One day, when I slipped up to his church to see what was going on, he suddenly emerged gorgeously attired in a silver paper tiara and a white cassock made from an old nightshirt, carrying a crozier made from a curved strip of wood which had been taken from a broken toboggan. He advanced towards me solemnly, pronounced a few mysterious phrases in loft Latin and made a number of gestures that seemed distinctly threatening. Then he informed me that he was the Pope and that I had just been excommunicated. He pointed to the stairs leading down from the attic and ordered me to descend into hell—in other words, to get out.

The schism was now complete between the church in the loft and the renegade I had become, so I confined my activities to the wood-shed, where there were plenty of interesting things to make up for the absence of my usual playmate. But we were still very fond of one another and didn't actually quarrel. Hervé always sat next to me at table and, in a low voice, used to tell me endless stories about saints and martyrs and missionaries. I would forget all about eating as I listened to him with my fork poised in mid air, absorbing a whole series of lectures on hagiography between the soup and the dessert courses. The rest of the family made such a noise talking that Hervé's remarks were overheard by no one but me. Sometimes my mother would glance over in our direction and ask, "What are you two so busy talking about?" Hervé would lower his long eyelashes over his blue eyes and reply, "Mother, I was telling Robert all about the catacombs where the early Christians lived. . . ." As a matter of fact, he used to tell me about lots of other things too, and one evening at dinner I was suddenly violently sick. Mother rushed over, picked me up in her arms and carried me off to my room. "Whatever can he have swallowed to get so sick without any warning?" she asked anxiously. What I had actually swallowed was a disgusting story about St. Benedict Labré who, according to my brother, made a practice of devouring the lice off his own body.

My mother was really very pleased to see these signs of a future vocation in her son. She was sure he was going to grow up to be a priest. As she was very devout herself, she already saw him in her mind's eye as a young curate, as a parish priest, and later, perhaps, who could tell, as a bishop. When she confided her secret hopes to my father, he shrugged his shoulders and said, "Just because a boy plays at robbers does it mean he'll grow up to be one?"

Hervé and my father didn't understand one another and didn't get on at all well. This mutual lack of confidence grew and grew until it finally developed into a real breach between them. My father's profoundly tolerant disposition and his horror of an open quarrel made him shrink from the very idea of talking things over with his son. He was completely nonplussed by the boy's behaviour and his bewilderment never decreased. Because of his natural indolence he never made the slightest effort to influence Hervé in his way of thinking. He just went on watching him rather anxiously from a distance. The boy was unusually sensitive himself, and so, of course, he was at once aware of this attitude of silent disapproval. It induced him to surround himself with a veritable network of defences, which gradually became an unassailable fortress in which he could go on living his rather mysterious life. My father, my two older brothers and my two sisters, who were all very down-to-earth people, preoccupied with concrete, material things, thought he was a bit mad. Hervé wasn't mad; he was just a dreamer.

Mother and I were his staunchest allies, and if Hervé may ever be said to have revealed anything of his enigmatic soul to anybody, it was certainly to us. Mother quite understood his religious exaltation and sympathized with his devotion to peculiar saints. As far as I was concerned, my brother's notions always filled me with intense curiosity. I was never tired of listening to him expound his ideas. My very deep affection for him was a powerful inducement to accept all he said as implicitly true, so I never questioned his highly romanticized version of the Catholic faith or his lyric accounts of the lives of the saints.

"When a person wants to be a saint," he said to me one day, "he has to start in very early to fast and flagellate himself and eat unpleasant things and distribute his possessions to the poor. St. Francis of Assisi used to roll about in a thorn-bush to subdue the flesh. . . ."

"Subdue the flesh? What's that mean, Hervé?"

My brother looked at me thoughtfully, but his handsome face was untroubled as he said, as if it were the most natural explanation in the world, "Subduing the flesh means killing the Devil."

I was all for subduing the flesh and killing the Devil, but I didn't much like the idea of the thorn-bush, so I asked if there weren't any other way. Besides, was it really necessary to be a saint? Our parents didn't go rolling about in thorn-bushes.

My questions only annoyed him and he just shrugged his shoulders. "Our parents are ordinary people and ordinary people don't roll about on thorns. They live a worldly existence."

"What's a worldly existence, Hervé?"

"You can't understand; you're not old enough. . . . But if a person wants to be judged worthy of receiving the marks of divine favour, like the stigmata of St. Francis. . . ."

"What are stigmata, Hervé?"

At that point he told me to go away and play in the wood-shed. He stayed on alone in the attic, reading his works of piety and his beloved *Lives of the Saints*, or acting out in solitude some episode constructed by his creative imagination. At one moment he would be Pope Anicetus saying mass in the depths of the catacombs, at another a Carthusian in his cell, or St. Francis preaching to the birds and fishes. He had a special predeliction for the lives of monks, and St. Francis was his favourite saint. He had made himself a whole set of monkish habits. I used to see him in a white robe with a black cowl or a brown one, or dressed as a Dominican, a Trappist, or a Benedictine. But the Franciscan habit was his favourite one, and he went about most often in an old brown, homespun cloak which he had made into a habit. He even carried his insistence on realism to the point of making a hood which he could pull down over his head. Then one day, when I had been invited to a solemn high mass, he appeared with a beard which he had made out of black wool stuck on to his chin.

His imitative zeal took him even further. He admired St. Francis of Assisi so much that he wanted to resemble him in every possible way. On one occasion, when he was playing out a scene from the life of his beloved saint, I looked on with wide-open, horrified eyes as he showed me his hands with a great red wound in the palm of each one. I couldn't help crying out in terror. I thought he had hurt himself, and rushed over to take his wounded hands in mine. A smear of red ink came off on my fingers, and Hervé seemed delighted that he had deceived me so successfully.

"Those are stigmata," he said.

This mania for dressing up and playing parts was mixed with a deep and sincere religious faith, but I wonder if he himself was ever able to separate what was imaginary from what was genuine. He played at a strange sort of make-believe all his life and never tired of masquerading in improvised costumes. He actually did become a monk one day and stayed a monk for several years. He may have been a bit of a saint too. At any rate we were destined to see him dressed in homespun with his head shaved and his bare feet thrust into leather sandals. Was he the victim of his own imagination in this instance? Was he still just playing at the same games which he had started in the attic? In any case, he suddenly left his monastery and returned to a "worldly existence," but he didn't live as ordinary people did. He could never have done that. He lived a secretive life, doing things which we knew nothing about and seeing people who were completely unknown to us. Every now and then he had fits of religiosity, and on those occasions he would go in for daily communion and regular attendance at early mass. These periods of intense exaltation would usually be followed by months of religious indifference, during which he appeared to be completely absorbed by the social whirl. I was already living in Paris in those days and used to get letters from him that were full of expressions of affection and confidence, though they sometimes included complaints and outbursts of self-pity as well. But I found it difficult to keep in really close touch with him; I knew too little about what he was actually doing. Yet, though I was far away from him then in every sense, I was still the affectionate younger brother who listened to what he had to say, and watched what he did, always full of wonder at his changes of costume or of attitude. I was still the devoted sailor, or perhaps more often the bewildered Paganel, for his innermost thoughts continued to elude me completely.

During one of my visits back to Canada, I found Hervé living in Montreal in a small apartment. He was surrounded by his collection of old furniture and old plate of which he was very proud. His day-to-day existence was what it had always been: vaguely mysterious. He seemed tremendously glad to see me and made a great fuss over me. There could be no question of my going to stay anywhere else; I must let him put me up. Then, when the time came to leave, and I climbed aboard the train that was to take me to the boat, he clung to me desperately and burst into tears. This highly emotional leave-taking upset me considerably and left me very worried. I didn't know what to make of Hervé, who seemed odder than he had ever been. A few letters from him reached me in Paris, and they were quite short, sensible ones. He complained a little about his health and said he couldn't see properly and had very bad headaches. Then, one day when I was expecting a letter from him, I got a cable from my eldest brother Roquebrune saying that Hervé had died quite suddenly.

In a letter he wrote me a few days later Roquebrune gave me some account of Hervé's last weeks. By that time he no longer ventured out-of-doors, as he suffered from spells of giddiness that frightened him. When the doctor came, he found his patient's blood pressure was alarmingly high, so they got in a trained nurse. His headaches by this time were almost unbearable and he had to stay in bed with ice-packs on his forehead. When he was delirious he babbled about strange visions. He seemed to be under the impression that he was still a monk and, when he looked at his hands, he thought he could see deep, red wounds in the palms. He died one morning, just at daybreak, in a moment of complete exaltation. Perhaps he thought he heard a voice calling him, or a summons of some sort. He got up in his dressing-gown and staggered a few steps across the room. Then the nurse came rushing up. Hervé gave a loud cry and collapsed in a heap. What was it he saw, or thought he saw? At the very moment of his death his imagination must have created a vision of that mysterious ideal which dominated him all his life.

Towards the end of the letter my brother remarked that they had only really discovered who Hervé's friends were at the time of the funeral. All sorts of very strange people—men, women and children, most of them very poorly dressed—turned up to walk behind the hearse. They were all in tears and seemed genuinely grief-stricken, and had gone together to buy a wreath of red roses which they laid on the coffin. Written on a card pinned to the flowers were the words, "To the Friend of the Poor."

After the funeral an old priest went up and shook hands with Roquebrune. He was the chaplain of the Society of St. Vincent de Paul. Hervé had been a member of this charitable organization and used to visit the poor and give them all he had: his money, his devotion, his friendship—perhaps even his life. Only this priest, and the poor themselves, knew anything about it. So Hervé, who dreamed of being a saint, who went about creating saints in his imagination, and who so often acted out their lives in make-believe, was perhaps, by virtue of his singular charity, a saint himself, though he may well have been quite unaware of it.

In our performances in the attic, I was always just the onlooker at a drama created by an imaginative boy. When the tales of the Orient and the adventures of explorers and trappers gave place to masses, when Sinbad the Sailor, Captain Hatteras and the fur-traders of the Northwest were ousted by a hooded monk or by a pope with a silver paper tiara, I lost interest in a dramatic form that had become too mystical for my taste. But by that time Hervé needed me no longer; he just went on acting out his play all by himself.

Children as a rule don't know what death is. I was born in an era of almost universal peace, at a time when there was little or no talk of wars and massacres. Wars were historical events that had happened long ago and there was no chance of their recurring. I had never heard of anyone we knew dying, and I got the impression that the people who were alive in the world around me would just go on living indefinitely. I knew old people died, but I thought they had to be very old indeed for that to happen.

Generally children get to know about death very gradually. Except in an age like the present one, when mass murder is an everyday occurrence, death doesn't have much meaning for a child. Sometimes I heard people say, "So-and-so has just died." But I didn't really know what dying meant.

Living the sort of sheltered life I lived, I could have no real conception of sudden and violent death. Yet that was precisely the kind of death that was suddenly revealed to me. The tremendous upset I suffered as a result was to be expected in the case of any child confronted with so violent a happening, and the fact that it involved Jacques, of whom I was so very fond, made the shock of my grief almost more than I could bear. Mother and Sambo knew how attached I was to Jacques, and so they tried to hide from me the fact, and particularly the manner of his death, but all their loving precautions were in vain. I had to experience the misery of bereavement and deal with it all by myself. Nobody could help me or distract me from it, not even Mother, or Sambo.

It happened one day towards the end of September. We were still having spells of warm weather and the garden lay basking in long hours of sunlight. There were still flowers blooming in the beds too. Over behind the house, near the wood-shed, the hen-run was still open and the hens themselves continued to wander about quite freely. The leaves were just beginning to change colour, turning red and gold. The first night frosts, though they were hard on the flowers, decked out the trees in brilliant shades.

I had been playing in the garden all that day. Sambo had been raking together into heaps the first of the fallen leaves, and the dogs and I loved rolling about in them. Then I went to pay a call on the cats, half asleep in the sun on the back veranda. I chased the chickens for a while, though this form of sport was strictly forbidden by Sambo, who claimed it frightened them and prevented them from laying. Finally I burst into the kitchen where Sophronie was sitting in her rocking-chair, knitting, and singing to herself in an undertone. I clambered up on to her lap and insisted on being told a story. The whole kitchen was fragrant with the odour of coffee, for Sophronie always kept the coffee-pot going on the back of the stove. Before starting in on her story, she heaved herself out of her chair and went and got a cup from the sideboard which she filled with a thick, black, well-sweetened brew. I asked for some milk and a piece of cake. When we had stoked up with food and drink, she and I set off together on our adventure with Sophronie supplying all the details as we went along. When the story was over, I shot out of the kitchen just as fast as I had shot in and went out through the yard to the garden to find Sambo and the dogs and cats, the piles of dead leaves and the sunshine.

My father drove back home towards the end of the afternoon. I rushed up to him, but he didn't seem to notice me and walked past me into the house. I dashed after him and found him in the dining-

room talking to my mother who was sitting near the big log-fire
burning in the fireplace. The few words I overheard rooted me where
I stood. I couldn't grasp their full meaning right away, but what I
did understand filled me with terror. Mother noticed me and made a
sign to my father, who stopped talking, but the words he had just
uttered still rang in my ears. What he said was: "I've just heard in the
village that Jacques has been killed in a hunting accident. They're
bringing his body back to the Simard place. . . ."

I knew Jacques had gone off several days before on a hunting trip
to the islands in the St. Lawrence. I even knew the very islands where
he had gone. You could see them from St. Sulpice, floating like long,
green shadows on the surface of the river. I had been out there once
or twice that summer with Jacques and my brothers. It meant driving
first to St. Sulpice where Jacques had a big row-boat that he left with
a habitant who had a farm along the shore. Hervé and I would sit in
the bottom of the boat, leaving Jacques and my two eldest brothers
to do the rowing. It used to take about half an hour to get there. The
river seemed to get wider and wider as we moved out into it. The
water was a calm, deep blue like the blue of the sky. Patches of
water-grass grew on hidden shoals that had to be avoided. Then the
prow of the boat would slide gently up on to the muddy bank. We
would usually stay out on the islands for several hours. Jacques and
Roquebrune and René liked to go in swimming. They were very good
at it and would swim far out into the river, but Hervé and I could
only swim like puppy-dogs, so we kept in close to the shore. Then
we always had a good lunch from the contents of the picnic-basket
Sophronie packed for us, and we usually ended up by going fishing.
For a long time I couldn't bring myself to put worms on a hook, but
I finally managed to conquer my aversion. Sometimes I succeeded in
pulling in a big, shining fish that went on quivering and jumping
about in the bottom of the boat. Occasionally, I would haul in a
little, flat, bluish creature or one coloured red and yellow. Jacques
taught me how to take them off the hook very carefully so that I
didn't prick my fingers. About sunset we would row home. The
bright colours of the long summer twilight mingled with those of the
blue-green water, which turned darker and darker with the fading
light. Sometimes a big paddle-wheel steamer, coming down from
Montreal, cut across our bows. Then we steered to face the wake
that only reached us long after the steamer had passed. Our row-boat
rocked up and down in the waves. At night, after I had gone to bed,

I still heard the sound of those waves, slapping hard against the boat, in my ears.

Jacques always went hunting on the islands in autumn. Flights of wild duck crossing the river used to stop and rest in the reeds. Jacques would hide in the boat with his dogs and lie in wait for hours.

My mother got up from her chair, took me by the hand and led me out into the garden. I said nothing. "Let's go and watch Sambo round up the chickens," she said. Bringing the chickens back into the hen-run was one of the old Negro's chores. He seemed to have a strange power over these undisciplined birds with their constant peeping and clucking. We walked over to the end of the yard, near the shed where Sambo was already busy rounding up the chickens. I always enjoyed watching this particular performance. Inevitably, there were one or two especially obstinate birds who rushed about like mad things with flapping wings and goggling eyes, so panic-stricken that they dashed past the entrance to their enclosure. Sambo would chase them and throw them up in the air so that they fluttered down over the wire fence into their own territory. I liked to see them spread their stubby wings and land delicately on the tips of their outspread claws.

Mother went up to the Negro and said something to him in English. He stared at her in astonishment and hid his face in his hands for a moment, then he looked over towards me. I turned away and went back to watching the chickens. I knew quite well what Mother had been telling Sambo. When she spoke English to him it always meant it was something to do with me and that she didn't want me to understand what she was saying.

Sambo kept me in the yard with him for a long time that evening. In one of the cart-sheds there was a swing and a set of nine-pins and a target with a bow and arrows. They were to keep us out of mischief on rainy days. It was the first time Sambo had ever taken me there to play in fine weather; usually he just let me run about in the garden. After an interminable time, Sophronie called us in to supper.

By the time I got to the dining-room, my father and mother had already taken their places. Aline and Henriette came in after I did, and then Hervé turned up. Roquebrune and René were the last to arrive. To come dribbling in like this, one after another, was quite contrary to our usual custom. The whole family invariably gathered in the dining-room a few minutes before the meal was served, and then took their places as soon as my mother was seated. That was the signal for Sambo and Little Sophronie, who waited at table, to come in with the soup-tureen and a pile of plates. The soup was put down in front of Mother and she filled the plates, which were then handed around by the two servants. It was always done this way. The fact that this procedure had been varied showed what a state everybody was in.

My father ate his food in silence and, in his case, this was very strange because he was always so fond of conversation. Mother seemed sad and preoccupied. Once or twice I caught her exchanging glances with Sambo. Henriette kept sniffling and blowing her nose, and one had only to look at Aline to see that she was on the verge of tears. My brothers had absolutely nothing to say for themselves, and that was pretty unusual too, because we were all encouraged to talk at meals, and everybody always shared in the general conversation, which was usually cheerful and sometimes quite noisy. Hervé always sat next to me and, as usual, he looked after me by cutting up my meat and peeling my apple at dessert. His long lashes were lowered, so I couldn't see his expression, but there were the same tears in his blue eyes as there were in those of Aline.

The meal was a hurried one; everybody just made a pretence of eating. Then my father got up and said to Mother: "I'm going over there with Roquebrune."

My mother said something to Sambo at the other end of the room on her way out, and he came over and took me by the hand and led me away. But we didn't go on out to the kitchen as we usually did. Mother didn't want me to be with Sophronie that evening. Sophronie would never have been able to control her feelings and would certainly have broken down. She loved Jacques as dearly as we did and was shocked and grieved by what had happened. Mother hoped to be able to keep me away from emotional scenes and to soften the blow for me as much as possible.

I went along with Sambo without any fuss and followed him up to his room in the shed. I was quite used to visiting him in his own quarters. He had quite a large room which he had fixed according to his own taste. The way up was by a ladder, and at the top were his bed, his stove and a movable bathtub, called a "sitz-bath," that looked like a big hat turned upside down on the floor. Everything was always spotlessly clean in Sambo's room, for he was a very neat and tidy person. He had covered a table with a piece of red velvet carpet that Mother had given him, and on this stood a statue of the

Virgin, a vase full of flowers, an oil lamp and his old Bible. Though he had become a devout Catholic, the old Negro clung to his Protestant Bible and read it with great fervour every night after he had said his prayers.

That evening it was in Sambo's Bible that I found forgetfulness and respite from the sorrow that clutched at my heart. The old Negro often let me turn over the pages of the big book, and I never tired of looking at the illustrations in it. I also liked listening to Sambo's comments on them. He knew his Bible inside out and could get really eloquent, in his own way, whenever he spoke about it. Sambo hadn't got Sophronie's creative imagination; he never invented his stories but always stuck to the facts. In his eyes, every word printed in the King James Version was irrefutably true, and he spoke of Abraham and Jacob and Moses and the Prophets as if they were close personal friends of his. Although Sambo's Bible was illustrated with woodcuts, he one day came to the conclusion that these needed livening up, so he added his own colour. He gave the Prophets a set of gorgeous robes coloured with red and blue and yellow and green crayons. Sarah was turned into a blonde, while Rebecca's plaited tresses became red. As for the angel who expelled Adam and Eve from Paradise, he brandished a sword that flamed like a rainbow with every colour in the box.

Sambo and I leant over the old book and looked at the pictures together. To my delight, he told me one of my favourite stories, the one about Abraham's sacrifice. I always got very alarmed about the fate of Isaac and was afraid God might not arrive in time to stay the hand of this terribly obedient father. Sambo's French was a sort of lisping sing-song and so, when he told it, the old legend sounded to me like a ballad. Every now and then he would break off to read me bits in English, just to prove that it was all there, set down in Holy Writ.

Later, when Sambo carried me back to my own room, half asleep in his arms, and I found myself in my own bed, my thoughts blended into a sort of dream peopled by the Biblical characters the old Negro had been telling me about. But the memory of Jacques was stronger than anything else, and I woke up crying bitterly. Mother rushed in to see what was wrong, and finally managed to sing and rock me to sleep again, but she realized that all the precautions she and Sambo had taken were in vain and that I knew perfectly well that Jacques was dead.

My mother sometimes went to visit an old lady called Madame Duplessis, who lived in a house standing all by itself beside the highway to Montreal. She always took me along with her, for this lady had a grandson, and Mother wanted me to make friends with him. It was thought that I hadn't enough playmates of my own age, and Mother considered she was doing me a favour by giving me a chance to spend the odd hour or two with this boy. But I didn't like Hyacinthe Duplessis at all.

His grandmother frankly terrified me, and I was even rather frightened of the house where they lived. So whenever I was told that we were going to see the Duplessis the next day, I used to feel rather upset, though I never showed it.

We would set off in the dog-cart with Mother driving. Jess trotted along cheerfully and we raised a small cloud of dust behind us as we went. I liked to watch Mother's gloved hands holding the reins. They moved to a regular, easy rhythm that matched the nodding of the mare's head. The road followed the bank of the river for a while and then turned sharply left. A narrow, tree-shaded avenue led up to an iron gate set in a fence. That was the end of the road.

Through the bars you could see an enormous garden with a house standing at the other end of it. I used to jump down and go and ring the bell. As I grasped the bell-pull that hung beside the gate I used to wish that they wouldn't hear me ring. But Madame Duplessis and her grandson were invariably at home, and as soon as the dog started barking, I knew we had been heard. Presently the dog himself would come trotting up and thrust his big, hairy head through the bars. As I stroked him, he would gradually stop growling.

Someone in the house down at the bottom of the garden always heard the bell. A window would go up and a woman would lean out from it. She always peered at us for a considerable time, as if uncertain who we were. It was as if the people who lived in the house were on guard against danger and feared the sudden arrival of some maleficent being. Perhaps, some day, the road that stopped short at their gate would give passage to an unwelcome visitor—the person whose arrival they so greatly feared.

My mother must have known something about the secrets of the Duplessis family, but my questions only got vague answers like, "Poor Madame Duplessis has a lot to worry about. . . ." It was clear I was to be kept in the dark. There were a whole lot of things like that that were never explained to me because they were "only for grown-ups." Once or twice I overheard my parents talking about the Duplessis, but I couldn't comprehend what they were saying. One day, however, my father said, "Poor Madame Duplessis may have got custody of her grandson Hyacinthe, but that wouldn't prevent. . . ." At that moment they saw me and stopped talking. Mother made a sign to him, and my father wound up the sentence by adding, ". . . you know whom from seeing him." That was all I ever managed to find out about "poor Madame Duplessis." But at least I knew there was some hidden danger threatening Hyacinthe.

Mother used to call out from the pony-trap, "Madame Duplessis! Madame Duplessis! It's me. . . . It's Robert and me!" Then the old lady would come down and let us in. She would first open the iron gate with a key that she took from a leather purse hanging from her arm. Then we could go up the drive. Before closing the heavy gate behind us, Madame Duplessis would take one or two cautious steps out into the road and glance in both directions, as if to make sure that there was nobody about. Mother would drive up to the porch, get down and tie the reins around one of the pillars of the veranda. I usually trailed along behind Madame Duplessis. Before going into the house with her caller, the old lady used to turn to me and say in a gentle voice, "You'll find Hyacinthe in the garden; he's over that way somewhere. . . ." Then she would wave an arm in the general direction of the walks and trees and flower-beds.

The dog and I would make our way slowly towards the other end of the garden. There was a thick wood there that marked the limits of the property. It was as if the whole world came to an end beyond those trees. In my imagination, they hid some precipice, some frightful abyss, where a land of evil things began. I knew Hyacinthe was somewhere in this wood. I would usually run into him when I least expected it, around a bend in the path.

He used to look at me with amazement and would appear to have forgotten who I was. Then, all of a sudden, he would start running and disappear among the trees.

I found this odd little boy rather frightening. He was a bit like some kind of small animal. He had long, fair hair almost down to his shoulders, and used to brush away a lock that kept getting in his eyes. Those eyes of his seemed to me the most disconcerting thing about him. The only human beings I had ever met before had either blue eyes or brown ones. My mother's eyes were grey-blue and Hervé's a deep blue, like the blue of certain flowers. My father and my two elder brothers had brown eyes. But whenever I managed to intercept a glance from Hyacinthe, I noticed his eyes appeared to be green.

I would run off after him and usually find him hiding behind a tree. Sometimes he crawled into a thicket or hid in the garden in a clump of flowers. As soon as I found him, he would run off again, and once more I would have to start looking for him. The dog had usually left me by this time to run along with Hyacinthe. This never-ending chase was the only sort of game we ever played, and I really quite enjoyed it. It used to go on until Madame Duplessis called us back to the house for our tea.

I don't remember Hyacinthe ever doing anything in particular but running and hiding in the garden or the wood. Very occasionally, he would stop for a moment to show me a plant or a flower or a seed and tell me what it was called, but then he would be off again and out of sight almost at once. This boy had only the wind and the rain and dust and grass and leaves to play with. He had never had any proper toys. The big, lonely garden, where he had always played, was his only resource and, because he was so accustomed to unbroken silence, he never shouted while he played. He remained quite silent all the time he was enjoying a game that he himself had invented and that he alone understood. He had no other company but his grandmother, and shyness made him run away whenever he suddenly found himself in the presence of a stranger. Yet I wasn't really a complete stranger, as I used to go and see him two or three times a summer. In spite of this, the only pleasure we shared was this exhausting and mysterious game which consisted of his flight, perpetually resumed, and my equally stubborn pursuit.

If I began to feel tired, and gave up the chase to sit and rest at the foot of a tree, he would never come back to look for me. For all he seemed to care, I could just stay there all by myself, gazing at the flowers, or the little insects scrambling over the hot, dry earth, or the green depths of the undergrowth. Sometimes a slight sound made me look up, but it always turned out to be just the chirp of a cricket or the peeping of a bird. I could be quite sure Hyacinthe would never call out to me.

Yet, when his grandmother called, he would emerge from his hiding-place right away and take me politely by the hand to lead me into the house.

Like many old-fashioned Canadian homes, it was a big, white-washed, wooden building. There was a row of rocking chairs on the veranda, but I never saw Madame Duplessis or my mother sitting in them. When we reached the drawing-room, we used to find them sitting beside small tables on which there were plates of cake and cups of tea. An old servant would then bring us steaming hot chocolate in big porcelain bowls.

The two women usually went on with their conversation, while my mother took a small fork and divided my cake in two. Hyacinthe ate his in silence. Sometimes I caught him looking at me and, when I did, I was curiously disturbed by those green eyes of his. When he looked at me, he never smiled, and after a few moments it made me feel embarrassed and I would turn away. He seemed to be scrutinizing me carefully, and this I found hard to bear. I felt those sea-green eyes of his going right through me.

After a while, I would get up and amuse myself by wandering around the two drawing-rooms, looking at the furniture, the pictures and all the various ornaments. Nobody ever paid the slightest attention to me. The two ladies went on talking in low voices, and Hyacinthe, who never moved from his chair, seemed lost in a day-dream as he stared out of the window.

Next to the room where we had tea was another one of much the same size. Between the two rooms was a door that was always left open. You had to be careful making your way about through all the furniture, because there was a great deal of it and it was scattered about in a very haphazard way. In the first drawing-room there were big sofas upholstered in red silk, and huge red easy chairs. In the second one the furniture was upholstered in yellow. White statuettes of women clad in long, folded robes stood on the marble-topped tables. I was astonished to find so many white objects around the place. I was particularly fond of looking at the framed engravings hanging on the walls. There were pictures of villas and churches and palaces from a world I knew nothing about. Mother told me one day that Madame Duplessis had travelled a lot in Europe many years before and that she had brought these engravings back from Italy. I imagine the white statuettes must have come from Italy too, but what I really liked best were the mosaics displayed in two glass cases in the second drawing-room. I would glue my nose against the pane and stand for ages gazing at the landscapes and figures fashioned out of little, many-coloured bits of stone. I envied Hyacinthe for having such a range of artistic objects in his possession, and such cunningly contrived ones too.

On the walls of the second drawing-room hung a number of framed photographs of an oddly-dressed young woman who always seemed to be standing in front of a monument or on the steps of some church. Later I came to realize that this must have been Madame Duplessis as a girl and that these photographs were taken during the course of her travels. I thought her very good-looking and when I went back to the other room, and looked at Hyacinthe's grand-mother, I found it hard to make out behind the wrinkles the young face the photographs showed.

One day, when I happened to be wandering about in the yellow drawing-room, I noticed a whole lot of photographs and coloured illustrations in the half-opened drawer of one of the marble-topped tables. I had got tired of always staring at the same objects and the same pictures each time I came, and so this was an unhoped-for diversion. I tipped out the contents of the drawer on to the carpet and lay down on my stomach to examine the treasure-trove I had just unearthed. These seemed to be more mementoes of Madame Duplessis' travels. There were pictures of towns and landscapes and castles that carried me off into a strange and wonderful world. One of the photographs slipped through my fingers on to the floor. At first, I thought it was another one of Madame Duplessis in her younger days, but then I noticed that the young woman smiling up at me under a huge picture-hat didn't have Madame Duplessis' eyes or mouth. But I had seen those eyes before somewhere. . . . Suddenly I recognized Hyacinthe's expression. The boy looked just like this woman in the picture.

I heard a slight sound and turned my head to look. Hyacinthe was there, standing right behind me. I had been so absorbed in my thoughts that he had come up close without my noticing. He leaned over, grabbed the photograph out of my hand and said with sup-pressed fury, but in a low voice, "You mustn't look at that!"

When Mother and I left, Madame Duplessis went down with us as far as the gate, and locked it carefully behind us. Hyacinthe was nowhere to be seen.

We didn't go to see the Duplessis any more that summer. I have no

E

idea why we never called on them in winter. So I didn't see Hyacinthe and his grandmother again for many long months. When next I rang the bell at the gate, and the old lady came to open it as usual, I could sense that something had happened. For one thing, the big dog didn't run out and bark at us. Madame Duplessis herself seemed even grimmer than usual. It seemed to me she looked up and down the road more anxiously than ever and took even more elaborate precautions in locking the gate. And when I reached the steps leading to the veranda, where my mother had got out of the carriage, Madame Duplessis didn't send me out into the garden to look for Hyacinthe.

This rather surprised me, and I stared at her not knowing what to do. I just stayed where I was at the foot of the steps while she and my mother went on into the house. Then the old lady turned back and beckoned to me. "You'll find Hyacinthe in his room," she said. "He hasn't been very well just lately, so I've kept him indoors."

A flight of stairs, covered with a thick red carpet, led upwards from the end of the passageway. I had never been to Hyacinthe's room before.

When I reached the top of the staircase, I found myself in a hall off which several rooms seemed to open, but their doors were all closed. I didn't know which was the right room. It seemed to me I must at all costs avoid making a mistake, and I was bewildered by all these closed doors. I preferred to leave any mistake to chance rather than to my own deliberate choice, so, pointing at each door in turn, I recited the rigmarole that Hervé had taught me and that we often used when we were playing games:

> Eenie, meenie, minee, mo,
> Catch a nigger by the toe.
> If he hollers let him go. . . .

Just then, one of the many doors opened, and there was Hyacinthe standing on the threshold. He was wearing his dressing-gown and had a book in his hand. He must have heard the almost inaudible sounds I made as I chanted the rigmarole under my breath. He looked at me with astonishment, and I, for my part, didn't know what to say. So we stood there looking at one another, not knowing what to do. After a few moments, he disappeared into his room, and I followed him in, though I hadn't been asked.

There was a big arm-chair in front of the window, and Hyacinthe went and sat in it. He still had the book with him and it lay open in his lap. The light was in my eyes when I looked at him, but I got the impression that his face was thinner and that he was paler than usual.

"Are you sick?"

He turned and looked out of the window at the garden and at the tops of the trees in the wood beyond. With one hand he absent-mindedly stroked the dog that was dozing on the carpet at his feet.

"No," he said. "No, I'm not sick, but Grandma doesn't want me to go out. I haven't been allowed into the garden for a fortnight, and I have to stay shut up in here. . . ."

He was silent as he gazed out at the garden again. Then he added, almost in a whisper, as if he were afraid that his grandmother might overhear him, "It's all since she got the letter. . . ."

Hyacinthe seemed to be talking for his own benefit rather than for mine. His words didn't seem to be addressed to anyone in particular, and he might just as easily have uttered them if no one else had been there. He probably had the habit of talking to himself and said a good many things like that when he was alone. I didn't ask him any more questions; he seemed so far away. After another long silence he said, "You can go out into the garden if you like. I'll call you when it's time for tea."

I went out of the room and down the red-carpeted staircase. As I went by the drawing-room door, I saw my mother and Madame Duplessis with their heads together over a sheet of paper that they seemed to be reading very carefully. I could just hear the sound of their voices. The old lady seemed to be reading aloud. They were so intent on what they were doing that they didn't notice me, and I managed to slip out without being seen. I imagined that what they were reading was the letter.

The garden was a blaze of colour. Madame Duplessis and Hyacinthe tended it with the help of their old servant. The little boy had learned all about looking after flowers from his grandmother. There was a great variety of them and some really beautiful ones among them. Great clumps of yellows, blues and reds stood out against the green of the lawn. I liked walking along the sanded paths and looking at the white-washed pebbles that framed the flower-beds. They formed a pattern in the garden which caught my fancy, so I strolled along quite circumspectly between the rows of white stones, stopping every now and then to look at some particular flower. Sometimes I would grasp one by its stalk and bend over a satiny lily or a silky peony so I could feel them against my face. These furtive contacts gave me a thrill. There were a few grains of saffran-coloured pollen on my lips and I wiped them away with my handkerchief.

Though I hadn't noticed where I was going, I had actually drifted over towards the iron gate. After all, I had just been ambling along looking at the flowers. Now I had reached the wooden fence that ran around the property and the tall gate was right in front of me. I looked up, and there, out in the road, was a woman staring at me.

I didn't know what to do and stood stock still in the middle of the path. The woman came over towards the fence and beckoned to me. She moved very gracefully and I felt greatly attracted towards this charming young person. She was unusually pretty, but I noticed that, though she smiled at me, her eyes, shaded by her broad-brimmed straw hat, looked very solemn. I was drawn slowly towards her, and soon there was only the wooden fence between us.

"I tried to open the gate but it's locked," she said. She went on smiling at me as she spoke, and now I could see that her eyes were green. "Open it," she said.

I ran over to the iron gate and tried to open it, but I couldn't manage. The young woman with the green eyes watched me anxiously.

"I haven't got the key," I said. "I can't get the gate open, Madame."

She frowned slightly, and for a moment her attractive face wore an expression of something approaching bitterness. I heard her say, "He calls me Madame," but she only said it under her breath.

"All right, leave the gate alone then if you haven't got the key and can't open it. Come over here where I can see you properly."

There was a note of command in her voice, though it was still full of tenderness. I felt rather frightened and at the same time curiously anxious to have a closer look at her. So I did what she said and going over to the fence, climbed part way up it. I was now standing on the crossbar, holding on to the pointed palings. This meant I could see over the top, and the young woman standing in the grass was on a slightly lower level. She reached up to me and pulled my head down towards her own. One of the wooden spikes of the fence was pressed against my chest, and I could feel it hurting me, but the kiss I received was so delightful that for a moment I paid no attention to the slight pain that accompanied it. The feel of this soft, velvety skin and the smell of perfume in my nostrils made it rather like being caressed by a flower, except that I had never been stirred so deeply by the touch of any flower. . . .

She released me at last but held my hands in hers as if to keep me from going. She kept saying, "Hyacinthe! Hyacinthe!" almost in a whisper. I pulled away from her and stepped down on to a flowerbed. Then, seized with a sudden panic, I started to run.

I ran as fast as I could right up to the porch and took the steps at a single jump, but at the door I stopped for a moment and turned around. The slender young woman was still to be seen quite clearly through the palings of the fence. She hadn't moved an inch.

My mother and Madame Duplessis were still in the drawing-room, and Hyacinthe came down a few moments later. Then the old servant came in with the tea things, and I drank my chocolate and ate my cake as usual. Once or twice I looked at Hyacinthe. He seemed thoughtful and very far away. I wasn't anxious to meet his gaze; all I wanted was to get away as quickly as possible. I had the feeling that at any moment he would find out what had happened, and it seemed to me that I had stolen a kiss that was rightfully his.

When we had driven the dog-cart through the gateway, Madame Duplessis looked up and down the road as usual before locking up. There was no one to be seen.

I was fated not to see Hyacinthe again for many years, and when I finally did meet him, it was in Venice, in very different surroundings. It was during my second visit to northern Italy, and I was thrilled to find myself in Venice once more, living in a fairy palace.

The Palazzo Dandolo is now better known as the Hotel Danieli, but the humbler use to which this noble dwelling has been put has not cheapened it to any appreciable extent. It still has its magnificent reception rooms and a staircase, all marble and gold, that makes the place seem as if it were still inhabited by a doge and his family. The dining-room is pure eighteenth-century Venetian and belongs to the most luxurious period in the history of this enchanting city. My bedroom had green painted panels ornamented with figure drawings.

I always get twice as much pleasure from being in a foreign city if I feel sure that nobody is going to come and bother me there. There is a feeling of great security in being alone and unknown among strangers. It is delightful to know that for the moment no one can make any claims upon me. Wandering about in the Palazzo Dandolo, I felt absolutely free and secure in my freedom. However, as a matter of fact, I had been seen and recognized.

One evening, when I was sitting in the drawing-room on the ground floor, looking out through the windows at the Riva degli Schiavoni, I noticed a man staring at me insistently.

The compelling nature of his gaze made me forget, just for a second, where I was, and I lost all sense of reality. I was suddenly no longer in Venice, in one of the drawing-rooms of the Hotel Danieli, but back in the Duplessis home at L'Assomption. Hyacinthe's green eyes! Those were the eyes staring at me now. I was so surprised that I jumped to my feet and the young man came over towards me. He hadn't changed much. He was tall and fair-haired and looked rather shy. Just as when I had known him formerly, he seemed both affable and absent-minded. He shook hands with exaggerated politeness.

"As a matter of fact," he said, "I'm not as surprised to see you as you are to see me. I knew you were living in Europe, and they told me at the Embassy in Paris that you had gone to Italy."

Hyacinthe and I looked each other up and down as we sat there smoking. I was very annoyed that he had spotted me. Venice was completely spoiled now as far as I was concerned. There, just on the other side of the shutters, the crowds were strolling up and down along the quay. The waters of the lagoon sparkled in the starlight, and gondolas came drifting out of the canals, all bound for the Piazza San Marco. In less than no time I could be in the Merceria or standing in front of the Palace of the Doges. Hyacinthe being there made all that impossible. As I listened to him talking, I was carried right back into the forgotten past. I sat there brooding about it when suddenly a remark of his made me sit up. "She died six months ago," he said, "and. . . ."

"She died?" I said. "Your grandmother? Madame Duplessis?"

He looked at me with astonishment before continuing. "I thought I just told you. My grandmother died two years ago. I was talking about Madame Duplessis, my mother."

There was a long silence after that, and in my mind's eye I could see again a garden full of flowers. I could feel the heat of a summer's day. I was standing at the fence and a wooden paling was hurting my chest because a young woman out in the road was holding me too tight in her arms.

"You never knew," Hyacinthe said thoughtfully, "you never knew that I lived apart from my mother and that she had lost her legal rights over me. She made my father very unhappy and so he asked my grandmother to look after me when he died. She became passionately devoted to me and for a long time she didn't even let me suspect that my mother was still alive. Naturally enough, one day my mother wanted to see the child she had abandoned, so she wrote the elder Madame Duplessis and asked for permission to visit me. She said she was going away, leaving Canada altogether, and she wanted to say a last good-bye to her son. I came across the letter among my grandmother's papers."

Hyacinthe told me all this in a subdued voice. I watched the smoke curling from the tip of my cigarette as I listened. I didn't dare look him straight in the face.

"I don't believe," Hyacinthe continued, "that my grandmother ever answered that letter. She had already got her lawyer to forbid my mother to come out to our place, but she was always frightened she might try. That's why she wouldn't let me go beyond the garden and why, sometimes, she even kept me indoors. I don't even know what my mother looked like, except for a photograph I found in a drawer in the yellow drawing-room. I don't think she ever dared to come and try to see me."

I got up quickly and said, "It's a lovely night. Let's go and walk along the quay as far as the Piazza San Marco."

"No," he said. "I'm tired and I've got to leave for Rome tomorrow morning."

We shook hands apathetically. Hyacinthe left Venice next day and I soon forgot all about the evening I had spent listening to him talking about the mother he had never seen and whose stolen kiss I had been the one to receive.

When I got back to Paris in the autumn, they told me at the Embassy that Hyacinthe Duplessis had been asking for my address. But I never heard from him and we never wrote.

Sambo must have been very old, though nobody knew quite how old, not even he himself. He was very tall, though a trifle stooped. His black skin shone like polished mahogany. His hair was quite white and stood out from his head like a tough, curly fleece. There was a gentle expression in the bright eyes that looked out from beneath his snowy eyebrows. He had a big nose, that was rather flat, and a huge mouth with very red lips. He was altogether a fine looking Negro. In the days of his youth, in Virginia, Sambo must have been cock of the walk in the Negro quarter of the small town where he grew up. When he played that banjo of his among the shanties, many a pretty girl in a cotton dress with a brightly coloured neckcloth must have felt her heart beat faster.

I didn't realize at the time that Sambo was a Negro. I could see he was black, but, as I had known him all my life, his colour never struck me as out of the ordinary. I found it as natural for him to have a black skin as for Sophronie to have a white one.

Sometimes, when we were sitting in the kitchen in the evening, Sambo would bring down his banjo and sing and play for us. He had a soft, rather twangy voice that sounded a good deal like the banjo itself. He sang us Negro melodies in a mixture of Virginia English and Louisiana French, a language full of strange lispings and sibilants. We couldn't hope to follow the songs word for word, but it was easy to tell from the expressive colourful tunes which ones were about love or fear, which ones were sung as supplications to God and which ones were to ward off devils. Sometimes the old Negro would get up and dance on the kitchen floor, playing and singing as he did so. Then Sophronie and Jacques and Godefroy and I would clap our hands to beat out the rhythm. Clapping hands as a musical accompaniment was traditional with the habitants of French Canada.

Many years later, long after Sambo's voice had been stilled, I heard Negro singers in the theatres of the Negro quarter of New York, but none of their songs ever thrilled me half as much as the ones I heard when I was a little boy, in the kitchen of the manor-house at L'Assomption. No Negro I have ever seen singing or dancing has moved me as much as old Sambo did with his banjo.

After Jacques' death, Sambo never sang again in the kitchen in the evenings. The autumn rains came drumming on the window panes, as the winds rose gustily outdoors. I used to come down and take my place at the big table in the middle of the room, next to Godefroy, who would be smoking his pipe with his elbows on the polished surface of the table. Sophronie and Sambo would be busy washing the supper dishes, while Little Sophronie tripped to and fro between the kitchen and the dining-room with dishes and cutlery. Nobody had a word to say and I used to get very bored. I never brought my book along now because Jacques wasn't there any more to teach me to read; I got my reading lessons from Mother.

The weeks that followed Jacques' death were terribly sad ones. We all missed him desperately during those evenings in the big kitchen. Once the dishes were washed and put away, Sophronie would go and sit in the rocking-chair near the table and knit in silence. I watched the play of the needles, fascinated, while Sambo dozed in his big wooden arm-chair. Little Sophronie had disappeared by now, as she had to get up at five to look after the cows. So she went to bed very early. As soon as Godefroy had smoked his last pipe, he too went off, to his room up in the shed. That left the three of us: Big Sophronie, the Negro and me. We were alone with the shadows cast by the chairs and tables and the tall cupboards. There was nothing to break the silence unless one of the dogs, asleep under the stove, began growling in his dreams. Sometimes you could hear the faraway sound of horses' hooves on the road in front of the house. I would look up in time to see the light from a lantern flash by each of the kitchen windows in turn. Then it would be quite quiet again.

I would clamber up into Sophronie's lap and she would start in on one of her stories. She kept her voice low in order not to waken Sambo.

Outdoors, the wind would start rising again, and you could hear the branches of the old elm trees in the driveway creaking and groaning at every gust. Big Sophronie would stop to listen for a moment and then go on with her story. Suddenly there would be a slight noise at the window, like something scratching, or a finger tapping on the pane. . . . It would rouse Sambo and cut off Sophronie abruptly in the middle of a sentence. We would sit there petrified, staring out into the night, waiting for something to happen. It was usually just a dried-up leaf, hurled by the wind against the pane. Sophronie would cross herself hurriedly, and Sambo would get up and lead me by the hand up the little back staircase that led from the kitchen to the top floor. When we got to my room he would undress me and put me to bed. He always used to stay for a while after that because I didn't like him to go before I got off to sleep. Mother would look in for a moment, kiss me good-night and vanish again. Usually the last thing I saw before dropping off was the big, shadowy form of Sambo receding down the passageway with his lamp.

When I woke up next morning, I would have forgotten all about the evening before. Each new day was the beginning of a totally new existence, just as if every single day was a complete life in itself.

When it rained during the night, and the garden was still wet, I would be sent to play in the shed, where the nine-pins were kept along with the swing, my bow and arrows, and my tin soldiers. I would spend hours there alone, quite busy with my own devices. The

F

cats, and Pipo and Porthos, the two dogs, used to come and keep me company. The shed had its own smell that mingled with the scent of the fields and the garden. It was a blend of hay and straw and mouse-droppings and old wood. Over in one corner stood an old carriage that had once belonged to Uncle Saint-Ours and was now gradually falling to pieces. The leather part of the collapsible hood had begun to flake away and horse-hair protruded from the cracks in the seat-cushions.

Along with the dogs and cats, I took innumerable trips in that old stationary carriage. Grown-ups don't understand children and don't realize that the things they enjoy playing with most are odd objects, which are really not meant to be used as toys at all. Whenever my father came into the shed and saw me sitting in the carriage, he would always look surprised and ask me what I was doing. How can a child explain why he likes doing some particular thing? But Pipo and Porthos and the cats understood perfectly.

From the driving-seat of the *calèche* I could see the yard and the whole back of the manor-house. Sometimes Sophronie would emerge from the kitchen to hang out the washing on the line stretched across the veranda, or Godefroy would come out of the wood-shed and cross the yard from one corner to the other with a basket full of logs. In spite of the curtained windows, I could even catch glimpses of my mother in the dining-room. My two eldest brothers were away at boarding-school and my two sisters and Hervé were up doing their lessons in the nursery-study with Mademoiselle Villeneuve. Everybody in the household was busy with his or her own affairs. I was free, in undisturbed possession of my own private world, and I knew even Sambo wouldn't come to fetch me away.

For some little time now the old Negro had been bed-ridden in his room.

Sambo was ill. Probably he had been ill for quite a while before that, but he had never said anything about it. Mother was the first to notice that the old Negro didn't seem well. One day at dinner she said, "Don't you think Sambo has changed?"

"Changed?" asked my father. "Yes, he has. He's quite white now; at least his hair is."

"He's all stooped over," said Aline.

"He's always been stooped," said my father. "But perhaps he's a bit more so these days."

"He's getting old," said Hervé.

"He's always been old."

"His hands tremble," said Henriette.

"Yes, that's it," said my mother, chiming in. "You can see his hands tremble when he passes around the plates. That trembling was what I first noticed. There must be something wrong. I'll ask Sophronie what she thinks about it."

When Sophronie was consulted she seemed rather surprised. She hadn't noticed that the old Negro didn't seem well. Though she was very fond of Sambo, she lived so close to him that she was unaware of the changes in him. So my mother decided to tackle Sambo himself.

"You'll have to take things more easily, Sambo. It seems to me that you're all tired out. Don't be in such a hurry to get up in the morning. Have you got pains anywhere?"

He drew himself up indignantly.

"Sambo ain't got no pains. . . . He ain't got no pains."

But he was ill all right. One day he stayed in bed and didn't come down. Godefroy, who had the room next to his in the shed, told them out in the kitchen that the old Negro wasn't feeling well. Mother climbed up the ladder to see what was wrong. She found him still in bed. He said there was nothing wrong with him but that he just felt terribly tired. So my father went up to see Sambo too, and took him a drink of rum. The old Negro was very abstemious, but he did appreciate a small shot of rum.

"We'll have to get Dr. Forêt in," said Mother.

"Maybe," my father replied. "But the trouble with Forêt is he's no good for anything but sore throats and child-birth. He'll take Sambo's pulse and say, 'He's got a sore throat; give him some potash.' Then where will we be?"

Sambo got a bit better and was in and out of the house again. He resumed his waiting at table, though his hands still trembled. Mother made him lie down in the afternoons, but he insisted on doing his regular work. All through that autumn, Sambo had his ups and downs. Then, for one whole week, he wasn't able to leave his room in the attic of the shed. He couldn't get up and found it hard to breathe. My father went off to fetch Dr. Forêt.

The kindly doctor gave him a thorough examination, and when he climbed painfully down the ladder Mother was waiting for him. Dr. Forêt didn't say that Sambo had a sore throat; he said his heart was weak. "Moreover, he's getting very old," he said. "You mustn't let him catch cold. A cold could easily turn into pneumonia, and with his heart the way it is. . . ."

Once again Sambo got a bit better. He would come down to the kitchen in the evenings to doze in his arm-chair. Sophronie made him take a glass of hot milk with an egg beaten up in it. According to her, it was a tonic that would "wake a man from the dead."

Right next to the kitchen, and leading on to the wooden veranda, were a number of rooms that had always been considered part of the servants' quarters. Both the Sophronies slept there. Mother wanted Sambo to move down into one of these rooms. She didn't like the idea of his having to cross the yard at night when it was raining. The shed and the stable and the cow-barn formed a little group of buildings at some distance from the manor-house. But the old Negro put his foot down; he liked the room he had in the attic of the shed, and he wasn't going to give it up. He felt safer up there with all his possessions: his statue of the Virgin on the table, his Bible, his stove and the carpet-bag which hung from a hook—the bag he had brought with him to Canada all the way from Virginia. Another room, or indeed any change of surroundings, would have put him off. Where he was, he could lie in bed in the mornings and hear the hens clucking in their coop. He could hear Little Sophronie come into the cow-barn and Godefroy moving about in the stable near by. He could even hear the horses whinneying, and could distinguish Jess the mare from Tiger by the clumping of her hooves. The dogs would rush barking into the out-buildings, and Godefroy would swear at them and chase them away. "Get the heck out of here, you devils!" This medley of sounds and voices was so familiar to him that he liked to have all that around him as he lay in bed, stricken by old age and illness. Death didn't seem quite such a threat to Sambo while there were all these signs of life about him.

Once again he came back to the house and seemed to be getting better, but the first spell of cold weather and the first snow set him back. He would hobble across the yard a little before noon, all muffled up in a long coat made of wild cat skins, with a fur bonnet down over his ears. Sambo had always disliked winter and couldn't stand the cold at all. He had never really become acclimatized in Canada and suffered from chilblains which Mother made him keep covered with grease. The African in him was always, to some extent, at odds with North America and, now that he was so old and weak, the cold and the snow frightened him. He felt he couldn't fight against them any more. Soon he had to stop coming over to the manor-house and spent all day in his room just resting. Godefroy took him up his meals and he would go along to see him. He was always delighted when we came and would sit up in bed with a happy smile. His skin seemed to have grown dull and pale, even by contrast with the white of the bedclothes.

I used to take the cats up to see him. He liked having them on his bed where he could rub their backs and sometimes pick them up to plant kisses between their ears, on their knobbly little foreheads. I also brought him up a hen that immediately started fluttering about the room in a panic. Sambo gave it bread crumbs which it pecked at greedily, its beak beating a voracious tattoo on the floor. The silly bird finally got tired of this and dropped down through the trapdoor. Sambo gave one of his creaky laughs which seemed to come from far down inside him. Hervé and I next decided to bring Pipo up, as he was the old Negro's favourite dog. It was rather a job to persuade Pipo to put his paws on the rungs of the ladder and start climbing. Even then, going up wasn't so bad, but the coming down part ended in catastrophe. Hervé was holding the dog by his hindquarters and I had him by his front paws. Pipo was quite a sizable dog and half-way down he got frightened and started to struggle, with the result that all three of us fell down the ladder on to the shed floor. There was no harm done, however, because there was a thick layer of corn-cobs spread out at the bottom to take care of possible accidents of just this kind. Godefroy was responsible for this precaution, as he had always been afraid that Sambo might miss a rung and fall and hurt himself. As a matter of fact, that had never happened.

We never stayed long with Sambo, as Mother had told us not to tire him out. His room was always very warm, for the stove was kept stoked up with logs and was practically red hot. A second stove was kept going down below on the ground floor of the shed. As soon as the really cold weather arrived, Godefroy banked snow up all around the outer wall. The big wooden structure, that looked rather like a Noah's Ark, was as dry and snug as could be. I moved my tin soldiers and my bow and arrows out there and played on the floor at the foot of the ladder leading up to Sambo's room. Mother drew the line at nine-pins, as they made too much noise, and she wouldn't let me bring the dogs in any more either. But the quiet, well-behaved cats were another story. They would come running out to me as soon as Sophronie opened the kitchen door, and, when I heard the patient cough, I would climb up with them to visit him.

Mother and my sisters used to come too, and would sit on the edge of his bed. Sambo was utterly devoted to my mother and tended to confuse her in his mind with the Blessed Virgin; the homage he paid my mother was almost a kind of worship. She used to tidy his bed for him and change his pillow-slips. When she got up to go, Sambo would take her hand in his and kiss it with great tenderness.

Sophronie was another frequent visitor, though getting up the ladder was quite a business for such a portly woman. In spite of her weight, though, she was very agile and nimble on her feet. She made it her job to get the old Negro to swallow chicken broth and egg-nogs and other concoctions capable of "rousing a man from the dead." But neither my mother's nursing, nor my father's tots of rum, nor Sophronie's delicacies could save Sambo from the embrace of death into which he sank a little deeper each day.

It was soon obvious that the old Negro was dying. Mother broke the news to us one evening; she realized it couldn't be long now. Sambo slept most of the time and only roused himself occasionally to drop off again almost at once. Dr. Forêt paid another visit, but his second examination only confirmed his previous diagnosis. The patient had only a very short time to live. My father made up his mind to go and fetch the parish priest next morning.

It had been snowing for three days on end and a great silence reigned over the whole countryside. The boundary fence, down at the end of the drive, had been almost obliterated. All you could see were the green balls on the end of the fence-posts, and even they were shrouded in white. The sound of sleigh-bells warned me that my father was coming back from L'Assomption.

He had hitched a team to the *berlot*. It was all Jess and Tiger could do to drag the sleigh along, as they sank in deep at every step. My father drove along slowly, sitting on the leather strap that served as a front seat. On the back seat was the Abbé Dorval, looking like a great bear, all wrapped up in his furs. My mother went to meet the priest at the front door, for he had the Blessed Sacrament with him.

The whole household went out with the priest to the shed. Getting the Abbé Dorval up Sambo's ladder was a complicated business. The old priest was very corpulent and his stomach got in the way when it came to climbing. Then his feet kept getting caught in his cassock, and he absolutely refused to let anyone else carry the black silk bag containing the Sacrament. My father climbed up ahead and gave him his hand to steady him. Godefroy brought up the rear and heaved gently at the right moments. Finally the Abbé Dorval reached the top.

The table near Sambo's bed had been covered with a fine damask cloth. Mother had also set out the three-branched silver candlesticks from the sideboard in the dining-room, and the candles were lit. Sambo's Blessed Virgin stood there with outstretched arms and in front of the statuette was a large crucifix. So that the dying man could keep his eyes on Christ crucified, Sophronie had propped it up against his Bible.

Sambo had been told that morning that the priest was coming. He was sitting up in bed, resting against a mound of pillows, and he opened his eyes as the priest appeared in the room. We all stood outside in the passage-way, and Mother had me by the hand. The Abbé Dorval said a few words to Sambo and then bent down to listen to what he had to say. The confession trailed off into a murmur and the priest made a great, sweeping sign of the cross over the old Negro who had closed his eyes again. Then we filed into the room and knelt down while Communion was administered to the dying man.

When we left, the Abbé Dorval said he would be back next day to administer Extreme Unction. Sambo seemed a bit better. He was able to make a few remarks and managed to swallow a little broth that Sophronie fed him from a spoon. But actually he was getting steadily worse, and, when my father got back from driving the Abbé Dorval to the village, Godefroy came in to tell him that the old Negro was dying.

I was out in the kitchen with Sophronie. The old woman felt too sad to say anything and left me to play with the dogs in silence. Outside it had stopped snowing and the garden, the yard and the shed roofs, all covered with fresh snow, were bathed in a pinkish glow. Each window in the kitchen looked out on a glittering fairyland. Then Godefroy came in. "He's passing on," he said.

This expression had a curious effect on me. I thought Sambo was going to come into the kitchen and that his soul was going to pass on out through the windows into the sunlight and the snow beyond. But Sophronie had understood the old peasant expression for dying. She threw a shawl about her shoulders and led me by the hand out to the shed.

My parents were standing by Sambo's bedside when I came into the room with Sophronie. Mother turned and looked at us and seemed to hesitate a moment when she saw I was there too. Then she drew me towards her. Sambo was lying there with his eyes closed, and his breath came with a slight rasping sound. His cheeks were hollow, and he looked older, much older, than I had ever seen him look. We stood watching him and waiting, but I didn't know what for. Then, all of a sudden, he opened his eyes.

Sambo was looking at us, and he could see us all without turning his head: my parents and Sophronie and Godefroy and me, the persons he loved most in the world, all gathered around him now. His face lit up for a moment with a half smile. Mother knelt down and took one of his old black hands with its pink palms between her own. Sambo's eyes took on a staring look. I could hear her whisper, "Lord, have mercy on him." After what seemed a long time, she got to her feet again, leaned over and gently brushed her hand over the dead man's face, closing his eyes.

Sambo the Negro was the first man I ever saw die. My old friend, who taught me so many things, taught me about death too. I saw life ebb away from his eyes and death take possession. Since then, every time I have encountered death, every time I have felt its presence near me, or I have actually witnessed it, I have thought back to the passing of my old Negro friend.

The course of my father's life was suddenly changed by a quite un- expected event, which modified the pattern of our whole existence. He was appointed private secretary to the Prime Minister of the pro- vince and had to go and live in Quebec when Parliament was in session. This meant he was away from home for long periods at a time.

This appointment dropped into his lap out of a clear sky; he didn't really want the job and he certainly made no move to obtain it. The Conservative Party had come into power and a cousin of my father's, Boucher de Boucherville, had been made Prime Minister. As my father took absolutely no part in politics, this occurrence didn't particularly interest him. However, he sent a letter of congratulation to Monsieur de Boucherville, who happened to be looking about for a private secretary. What he needed was a man of the world with nice manners and a good presence. One evening, Godefroy, who had been to the village and looked in at the post office, came back with a letter which he left on the table in the hall. Letters were always put there, though they sometimes stayed there for days at a time without any-one bothering to open them. My parents were never in any hurry to read their mail. They didn't think the letters that came to the house could bring them any special news, any unlooked for happiness or anything else of importance. They had been completely absorbed for so long in each other, in the children, and the house, that anything coming from outside their little world left them quite indifferent. Yet it so happened that the letter waiting downstairs on the table in the hall was destined, though it was only a few lines long, to change our lives completely. Monsieur de Boucherville wanted to know whether my father would like to be his private secretary.

We were just sitting down to dinner when my father opened the letter. He had picked it up absent-mindedly on his way through the hall. It had been lying there on the table for two or three days at least. He read what his cousin Boucherville had to say, looked a bit startled and then read the letter through again before remarking, "That's a queer notion."

"What is?" asked my mother.

"Here, read it for yourself."

The letter was passed around the table till it reached my mother. She read it and then put it down beside her plate without saying any-thing. My father, for his part, was busy carving a chicken and seemed to have forgotten all about the incident. Though he was an intelligent, well-educated man, he was very easy-going and all he asked for was to be left in peace. It had simply never occurred to him to use his family connections to get himself a government job. Though he wasn't wealthy, he had a large enough income to allow him to live happily with his wife and children in the manor-house at L'Assomption. His father had left him a small nest-egg, his maternal grandfather, Hertel de Rouville, another, and his great-uncle, La Broquerie, still another. The seigneuresse had also left my mother a small nest-egg. All these nest-eggs mounted up to a sizable sum. Besides, later on, my parents inherited money from Cousin Glen and Cousin Hermine. So my father had finally got into the habit of imagining that there would always be some elderly relative at death's door just on the point of leaving him a small nest-egg. On one occasion he was even willed a sum of money by an old gentle-man who wasn't even related to him. This was a Monsieur Dumont who had been Hertel de Rouville's agent and had managed his seigneurie as well as the one my father inherited. It may be that

Monsieur Dumont hadn't always been strictly honest, because when he died he left my father and Uncle Rouville fairly large sums of money, and the cash was handed over by a priest who had been the old reprobate's confessor. In any event, the effect of all these bounties had been to convince my father that he could count on a gentle but steady rain of gold from heaven.

My mother had been rather worried about money matters for some months. There was a depression in Canada about 1890. One bank had to close its doors and a certain number of businesses went bankrupt too. My father lost a lot of money and much of the stock he held was worthless. It meant a lessening of his income. At first he was rather worried about it and got depressed and out-of-sorts. But after a while he stopped brooding and finally forgot all about it. But my mother couldn't stop worrying. She was anxious about our future. Her four boys and two girls couldn't go on living forever in the manor-house at L'Assomption, with their lives bounded by the back yard and the front garden. One fine day these six beloved children would have to go out into the world, and she wanted them to be happy. The world meant everything beyond the immediate horizon: Montreal, the province of Quebec, all Canada for that matter. When she got up from the table that evening, my mother swept us all with a long, lingering look. Then she picked up Cousin Boucherville's letter, went over to my father, put one arm lovingly round his neck and led him out to the drawing-room.

It was only much later that Mother confided to me what was said on that occasion. When she got to be a very old lady, she liked talking about her earlier life and, in particular, about her younger days and about the husband she had loved so deeply. When she was nearly eighty, and he nearly ninety, her face would still light up with an expression of great tenderness whenever she glanced in his direction. In her eyes, he was still the good-looking cousin who was introduced to her one day back in 1874. She often told me the story of that particular day, which proved such a happy one for her. She was just twenty and he thirty when they met for the first time. Though they were related, they had never met, for the simple reason that my mother at that time never ventured very far from the manor-house at L'Assomption. There had been a number of suitors already, but the old seigneuresse—the lady of the black lace bonnet in Hamel's portrait—was a difficult person to please and wanted her niece to make a really good marriage. One young man, a Monsieur de

Beaujeu, was on the point of being approved as a suitable candidate. "He had nice manners," my mother used to say. It was apparently the only thing she noticed about him. Then, one summer's day, Grandfather de Salaberry came out from Montreal with another young man in tow. "This is a cousin of yours you have never met," he remarked as he introduced him to his step-daughter. When she reached that point in the story, my mother would always go over to her writing-desk and take out a little casket in which she kept letters and photographs. She would take out a post-card size picture and hand it over to me with the words, "See, this is what he looked like." The picture showed a slender, dark-complexioned young man wearing a grey suit and holding a top hat in one hand. She seems to have been quite dazzled by this handsome young man the moment she first laid eyes on him, and, during all the fifty-eight years that she was married to him, she never managed to get over it.

They had been married for about fifteen years when the Boucherville Ministry came into power, and those early years of their long married life were certainly the happiest ones. My father got the idea that all he had to do to prolong this state of affairs indefinitely was to remain passive and not be too ambitious, but my mother was full of foreboding for the future and felt that there were dangers ahead. While they went on living their ideally happy life together, cut off from the rest of the world, times changed. Their financial losses were one indication, at least to my mother, that this was so.

It seemed to her that Cousin Boucherville's letter deserved an answer. She told her husband so, stressing practical considerations such as the state of their finances. Women who are very much in love can often be quite realistic about things. This combination of seeming opposites is often encountered in mystics, in people who see visions and converse with God and receive stigmata, but who, at the same time, build monasteries, found religious orders and draw up their statutes. This is particularly true of the women who have been mystics. St. Theresa used to tear herself away from the embrace of God to check the convent's account books. On this special evening, my mother spoke of the deficits from our own household accounts as she embraced the husband she loved so dearly.

My father was a little annoyed, but my mother's arguments were convincing, and so he went off to Quebec. We all stood on the porch together to watch his carriage turn the corner out of the drive. Just as he passed between the two posts, surmounted by green-painted spheres, he looked around at us and saluted Mother with a flourish of his hat. She replied with a timid wave, and then the carriage passed out of sight along the road to the station.

We all knew Mother had been upset by my father's departure. It was the very first time they had ever been separated and this made it doubly hard for her. As a matter of fact, she began looking forward to his return the moment the carriage disappeared down the road, and she couldn't help worrying a little about his forthcoming meeting with the Prime Minister of the province. She knew Monsieur de Boucherville only slightly, and my father's cousin had the reputation of being aloof and arrogant and altogether a rather difficult sort of person. He lived over on the other shore of the St. Lawrence, almost opposite us, in a village which bore the same name as his own. My father, before his marriage, had been in the habit of spending a good deal of his time at Boucherville, where he stayed with his old uncle La Broquerie. The patronymic of both the La Broqueries and the Bouchervilles was Boucher and they were branches of the same original family. But for some years my father had been almost out of touch with his cousin Boucherville, just as he had lost contact with almost all his relatives and boyhood friends. My mother couldn't help remembering too that my father was unpredictable and capable of being every bit as arrogant and haughty. If he didn't happen to like the Prime Minister, he might easily tell him to go to the devil. Then a letter arrived from Quebec.

This particular letter wasn't left lying about on the table in the hall downstairs. As soon as Mother heard that it had come, she rushed down to open it and stood reading it on the spot.

Romantically-minded people are easily stimulated by the merest trifle. My mother was convinced that the very absence of her husband constituted a fresh bond between them. Never before in her life had she had to conjure up his appearance and his gestures in her imagination, because never since their marriage had they once been separated. He had been gone for two whole days now, and she must have been brooding about him and remembering what he was like. There in her hands was a letter that brought him back to her.

I interrupted her just at this moment, for I came running down the hall. I stopped suddenly when I saw her, but apparently she neither saw nor heard me. She just stood there holding the letter, reading and re-reading certain paragraphs and sentences. The hall was dimly lit by a small fanlight above the front door. My mother stood silhouetted

against what little light there was, with her crown of fair hair gleam-
ing. She was a rather tall woman, and she seemed to loom even taller
than usual in this shadowy light. I went up to her cautiously and
touched her arm. She smiled but went on reading. Then suddenly she
noticed I was there and, dragging herself with a great effort from her
thoughts and the letter that had aroused them, she knelt down beside
me so that our faces were on the same level. I remember noticing the
rustle of her skirt on the tiled floor. Then she took me and hugged me
and covered me with passionate kisses. But though on that occasion
she kissed her son, I believe it was her husband that she had in mind.

It was a very optimistic letter, full of good news. The Prime
Minister had been most gracious and seemed delighted that his cousin
was willing to act as his private secretary. Monsieur de Boucherville
had thought of him in the first place because he knew he had no
business or professional ties and because he wanted a man who
could be treated as an intimate and in whom he could have complete
confidence. The old French-Canadian traditions of kinship and
family loyalty were still maintained in French Canada in those days.
People were in mourning for very distant relatives and shared the joys
and sorrows of persons they hardly knew and whom they saw only at
long intervals. Being somebody's cousin was a relationship that really
counted for something. French Canada had preserved the system of
nepotism that in France had turned the monarchy and the church
into one vast family concern. Just as kings made their brothers
governors of provinces, and popes gave cardinal's hats to their
nephews, so French-Canadian ministers were in the habit of giving
jobs to people whose sole claim was that they and the minister had a
great-grandfather in common.

In the nineties, the provincial capital was still very much what the
old colonial capital had been, with its reminders of the past at every
turn. The streets had hardly changed at all in appearance since the
days of the last Marquis de Vaudreuil. Even the newer houses dated
back to the time of Lord Dorchester and Sir James Craig. The
Quebec of the Boucherville régime was still an authentic antique; the
spurious Château Frontenac, designed to titilate American tourists,
had not yet been erected. The *calèche* was the type of conveyance
everybody used and not just a quaint amusement reserved for visitors
from New York or Chicago.

Quebec society had remained intact too; more than that of any
other city in the province, it had retained its special virtues, its pre-

judices, its defects and its charm. It was an aristocracy of townspeople as old as the colony itself. Its leading families had pretentions to nobility, and their presence created an atmosphere that blended perfectly with the old private residences of the Rue d'Auteuil or with the handsome houses that lined the Rue St. Louis and the Rue des Remparts. The persistence in late nineteenth-century Quebec of this old French-Canadian social fabric was a kind of miracle of survival. But like the old château of the French governors, whose ruins topped the cliff, this society was soon destined to disappear completely, leaving only a memory behind.

Even in political circles, a rather outmoded politeness and exquisite manners were still considered indispensable. Conservatives like Monsieur de Boucherville, Sir Réal Angers, Sir Adolphe Chapleau, Monsieur Boucher de La Bruère and Monsieur Chauveau or liberals like Monsieur Letellier de Saint-Just, Sir Wilfrid Laurier, Monsieur Honoré Mercier and Monsieur Joly de Lotbinière were all excessively polite. Debates in the Quebec parliament were conducted like a discussion in a drawing-room. An Englishman, who on one occasion attended a session of the Legislature, remarked, "The French Canadians are a race of gentlemen."

All civilizations reach a peak which is inevitably followed by a complete revolution in manners, morals and customs. No society can remain at its apogee for more than a very few years, and refinement is always the end product of a long series of social accretions perpetuated by tradition. It takes several generations of civilized persons to produce intellectual subtlety, purity of diction and consummate politeness. By 1890, French Canada could look back on two centuries of civilization of a rather exceptional quality. The traces of this civilization are still to be found in surviving examples of the architecture of that day, in country churches and fine old farm-houses, for even the peasantry was not excluded from a spiritual climate that was all-pervading. The habitants had the same good manners, and it was another Englishman who remarked at this time that "one can always distinguish a native of the province of Quebec by his French courtesy." Some traces of this vanished civilization still persist in a few families, just as there are a few fine houses and churches, built in the old French-Canadian style, still standing. But these remains are only archaeological curiosities, museum pieces at best. The towns and the countryside of the province of Quebec are thoroughly Americanized, and the people who live there now don't even suspect that their ancestors built up a delightful civilization which was still in existence a bare half century ago.

My father thoroughly enjoyed his new life. He was a society man at heart and he now came into his own. Before his marriage, in the days of his youth in Montreal, he had flitted from drawing-room to drawing-room and had frequented a great number of banquets and balls and theatre parties. He sometimes used to tell me stories about this gay period of his to which he looked back with a certain regret. He had become a member of a club that was renowned for its elegance, and he used to spin yarns about his friends Raoul de Beaujeu and the journalist Achintre and the girls they knew. He used to tell us too about the parties at carnival time and about all the petty scandals that went the rounds of the drawing-rooms involving the women who "got themselves talked about." It all sounded very brilliant and wonderful in the remote calm of the manor-house at L'Assomption. As my mother had never had any contact with the world of fashion, she never tired of hearing my father tell these stories.

In Quebec, he picked up where he had left off. He was soon very much in demand and accepted invitations right and left. He found his work with the Prime Minister—or Mr. Premier, as everybody called him—quite fascinating. He discovered too that he had a knack for politics and, though these were only provincial politics, they were quite complicated enough. His chief found him very useful and was more than glad he had offered him the job. He particularly appreciated my father's tact and his sense of timing. All in all, my father got on famously in a world full of secrets of state and complications of one sort and another. Monsieur de Boucherville was a rather straightforward sort of person, anything but devious, and, like most conservatives of the old school in his day, he was a great stickler for principle. His secretary was often able to give him very good advice based on an instinctive sense of diplomacy and a knowledge of human nature that went well below the surface. When he had been Prime Minister on a previous occasion, Monsieur de Boucherville had had an involved dispute with the Lieutenant-Governor of the province, Monsieur Letellier de Saint-Just. The affair had led to a veritable palace revolution that did the Conservative Party a good deal of harm. My father believed that incidents of this sort were best avoided and took pains to round off the sharp edges of ministerial policy. But the social life of the little capital interested him even more than the complexities of party politics.

His letters to Mother were full of social gossip. He told her all about the dinner-parties that various cabinet ministers had given, about the Cardinal-Archbishop's receptions and about all the drawing-rooms he frequented. Whenever the Prime Minister entertained, he had a lot of work to do, because his chief didn't really understand questions of protocol and the correct seating of his guests at table. As my father once wrote, "Protocol is just as important here as it ever was at Versailles in the days of Louis XIV. Democratic society is just as jealous of its privileges as feudal society was. A member of parliament's wife, who is incorrectly seated at table, can give a scowl as black as any duchess who is received in audience by the king and finds no stool placed ready to support her backside." He used to claim that Quebec under Monsieur de Boucherville's government was as hard to rule as the entire British Empire under Queen Victoria.

These letters made my mother more and more unhappy. It wasn't that she was jealous or that she doubted the fidelity of the man to whom she was so devoted. She was completely certain of his love and loyalty. The very idea of doubting him would have appalled her. What distressed her was his absence and the fact that it looked as if he were going to remain away a long time. He obviously couldn't come home before the session was over. Saddened by their separation, she became pensive and absent-minded and full of melancholy. Even we children couldn't hope to fill the gap that had been left. She looked after us and she looked after the house, as she had always done, but her thoughts were elsewhere.

Then one day a letter came that filled her with happiness; he was planning a trip home and was going to stay two whole days. She literally bloomed before our eyes and at once became intensely active again. She scurried around the house giving orders about this, that and the other thing. First of all there had to be a great house-cleaning. Godefroy dragged all the carpets out into the yard and gave them a thorough beating. Then all the furniture was polished with great vigour. The mirrors were rubbed over with chamois-leather and all the silver was cleaned. Out in the kitchen, Sophronie baked cakes and made head-cheese and maple-cream. Even the dogs were bathed and brushed, and Godefroy was given special instructions about the grooming of the horses, since they would meet my father's eye the moment he arrived.

She went to meet him at the station. I happened to be playing in the garden when they drove up, so I rushed out. Mother was driving

and looked absolutely radiant with happiness. She held the reins in
her gloved hand and beamed at us. She had a big green felt hat on
over her fair hair. To look at her you would have thought that her
husband who sat there beside her had been rescued from prison or
had just returned after a long and terrible exile.

For two whole days the household reverted to its former pattern.
Godefroy went to fetch Roquebrune and René back from school, so
we were all there. There were no gaps around the family board and
mealtimes were as cheerful and as lively as they had ever been. My
father had come back with a great fund of funny stories and *risqué*
remarks, and we listened to him enthralled.

He made a tour of the property and resumed contact with all the
various people and farm-animals and miscellaneous objects about
the place. Wherever he went Mother went too. From where I was
playing, out in the wood-shed, I could see them sauntering about in
the garden. My mother held on to my father's arm and walked with
her face turned up towards him, listening to everything he had to say.
Then they strolled back towards the house and went into the drawing-room by way of the french windows. As they did so, he stood
aside to let her go in ahead of him. She held her skirts gathered in her
left hand, as women did in those days. When she released it, her train
rustled on the floor behind her as she walked.

Those two days went by very quickly. Then he was off again, but
this time Mother didn't go to the station. We all waved good-bye
from the porch. Just as on the previous occasion, the moment the
carriage reached the end of the drive before turning into the highway,
he turned and took off his hat to my mother and she made an almost
imperceptible sign in reply. But this time I noticed it was a kiss she
sent him.

He came back home on other occasions later, indeed whenever the
session allowed him a few days' respite. He seemed to be always using
the word "session." We knew that when the session was really over
he could come home to stay. Sometimes he turned up on autumn
evenings and sometimes on winter nights. Mother always went to
meet him at the station. Sometimes he could only stay a few hours
before going off again. When he had gone, the house became sad and
silent and as if deserted once more. Godefroy would drive my older
brothers back to their boarding-school. For Hervé and my sister it
meant going upstairs again to the schoolroom to resume their
lessons with Mademoiselle Villeneuve. Big Sophronie, out in her

kitchen, went back to baking a kind of cake we called "black cake." It had nuts and raisins in it and I didn't like it very much, but we had it week after week.

Towards evening, when I stopped playing for the day, and the dogs and cats had taken refuge in the kitchen, I would invariably rush into the house. When I wanted to find Mother and put my arms round her neck and talk to her, I could always be sure of finding her in the dining-room, seated beside the fire-place. She would have a book lying open in her lap or would seem to be busy with a piece of needlework, but she was never really doing anything; she was just sitting there, listening, gazing at the burning logs. Another waiting period had begun.

A person's life is made up of a whole series of coincidences and purely fortuitous events. Biographers who write the "lives" of famous persons generally manage to give the impression that the careers of their heroes developed logically, but then books are always easier to plan than human existences themselves, and literary artifice can alter the actual facts a good deal. That is why the lives of great men are so misleading. Even when the biographer manages to obtain access to the great man's letters and private papers and gets to know some of his secret thoughts and perhaps the main body of his ideas, a host of details will still elude him, as will, perhaps even the one decisive factor in the man's life that no one knows anything about and that passed completely unrecorded. For these reasons it is impossible to write another person's life with complete fidelity, and this applies just as much to the lives of the great as it does to those of humbler folk. One can really only write one's own life.

I think if my father had ever sat down to write his autobiography, he would have described the letter he received from his cousin Boucherville as the really decisive factor in his career. This single sheet of paper gave the signal for an abrupt change of direction, a complete about-face. For nearly fifteen years he had lived an untroubled existence with one day very much like another. He had surrendered to the charm that such a life can bring, and he was happy. Because he loved his wife and children, he never noticed that he was gradually getting bored.

But the fact of the matter is that he was really getting bored.

My mother had never known anything but country life. Because she had never lived anywhere else, it seemed to her perfectly natural to go on living in the country permanently. She had the land in her blood and was devoted to the property and, in particular, to her garden. She even did a little buying of land on her own, to add to the estate and round it out. During all those years it had never occurred to her that she and the family could possibly live anywhere else than in the old manor-house with its trees and its garden beds and its domestic animals that taken all together made up her children's heritage. My father was country-bred too; he was born in the manor-house at St. Hilaire, which had belonged to his grandfather, Hertel de Rouville, and he spent his childhood at Rigaud in a big white house belonging to his father which stood perched on the hillside. But the memories of these early years meant nothing to him. Before he had finished growing up, the fine house at Rigaud was sold and he went to live in Montreal. He took with him no special affection for the hills around Rigaud nor for the big, impressive rooms of the house where he had lived as a child. He had far happier memories of St. James' Street, of Notre Dame Street and of La Gauchetière Street in Montreal. These were the fashionable streets in his day. The stories he used to tell us about his youth always concerned events which had happened in that particular part of town. His friends all lived there, his tailor and his bootmaker had their establishments there, and his club and the theatres were also in that area. He had merely accepted country life for his wife's sake. But it did have its irritating aspects, and when his boredom showed in his expression and my mother began to get worried about it, he used to say, "Yes, of course I'm annoyed, but it's because your tenant-farmer's been cheating us again."

Though the country got on his nerves, he would never have made a move to leave it of his own accord. Like many intelligent, observant people, he was just a little lacking in imagination. To rouse him from his particular form of indolence, something had to happen with which he had no direct concern. The letter was quite providential in this respect. My mother was at once instinctively aware of the possible consequences, and she realized too that the future was a threatening one. She was going to lose all those things she cherished so dearly: her house, her garden and the farm lands that went with them.

The Boucherville government seemed to be running into stormy weather. My father, in one of his letters, gave us to understand that the ministry wasn't likely to survive much longer. My mother didn't know whether she should be glad or sorry about it all. She wanted him to come home more than she had ever wanted anything in the world, but she felt it was a pity that his career should be cut short so soon. But then another letter arrived with very important news. My father had been selected for a civil service position in Montreal. He went on to explain that there was nothing out of the ordinary about this and that he hadn't been granted any special favours; it had always been the custom for an outgoing Prime Minister to find a government job for his private secretary.

My father was delighted. When he came home to the manor-house he brought further details about the position he was going to take up in Montreal. He was to have an office in the Court House and his job would be to supervise all Government purchasing. He would have to be on the look-out to see that the contractors didn't meddle with their accounts. On his way through Montreal he had gone to have a look at a number of available houses and flats. He thought it would be a good idea if we went to live in the St. Louis de France district, as he had a lot of friends there. He told us all this at dinner that evening, mixing up these plans and details with stories about Quebec, the forthcoming collapse of the Government and various cabinet ministers and members of the legislature. He hadn't a single word to say about the manor-house or the farms or the servants or the stock and seemed to have completely forgotten their existence. He behaved like an officer who had just received a new posting. He was off again with his wife and children and had no regrets to spare for the place he was leaving. He seemed to have no ties with special places or physical objects. His ancestors had all been soldiers and it was from them that he had inherited his remarkable adaptability, that foot-loose quality that made him ready and even eager to pull up stakes and go. His very first Canadian ancestor, a former *Mousquetaire Noir*, had come out to Canada in Louis XIV's day, in Contrecœur's company, and he had had to give up first his native Gascony, then Paris, and finally France itself, without once looking back.

It was a very different matter for my mother. She was deeply attached to her surroundings. The new home she was going to would seem terribly alien. She had no fondness for social life, and she realized she would have to meet many people and pay calls and do a certain amount of entertaining. Being naturally shy, she shrank from the very idea, but it was when her thoughts turned to the manor-house and Sophronie and the horses and the garden that she felt really desperate.

Everything had to be sold. It was no use keeping up a property that would just become a burden. My parents talked the whole matter over. My mother had a vague idea that they might be able to keep the manor-house and the garden and just sell the farms and so get rid of the tenant-farmer who "robbed us." Then we could come back in summer for the holidays. But my father managed to convince her that the plan wouldn't work. He totted up figures and talked a lot about investments. It appeared he had already started to make arrangements for the sale. There was a chance of making a good thing of it. Somebody had offered to take the property off his hands in exchange for a block of three houses in Montreal, in the St. Henri district. Once before my father had concluded a similar deal when he had sold his house and land at Rigaud and had become the owner of some real estate in the St. Jacques district. Montreal was expanding rapidly and was on its way to becoming a really big city. This meant that rents were bound to go up. His arguments were based on hard facts and he buttressed them up with a lot of talk about income levels and reinvestment.

Mother finally agreed with him. She would have agreed in any case, even if he had suggested going to live in the Rockies or on the Island of Anticosti or had wanted to exchange the old manor-house and its farms for a settler's cabin in Manitoba. She would have followed him to the ends of the earth. Leonardo da Vinci must have had a woman like her in mind when he spoke of beings whose love is imprisoned in their eyes.

After all, Montreal wasn't at the other end of the world, but to my mother the very name of the place symbolized the great unknown. She had lived there for a short time just after her marriage, but she had never really got used to it and was delighted to go home again. She knew only too well that she would feel completely dispossessed once she was separated from her house and her garden with its trees and walks. Women have a stronger feeling for possessions than men have. All that real estate in the St. Henri district could never be a substitute for the place where her affections had always been centred.

Still another fatal step would have to be faced very soon. The two Sophronies and Godefroy would have to go. Parting from Old Sophronie meant a very special wrench. And how was the news to be broken to her? The old servant was now well past seventy. She had lived in the manor-house all her life and was as much a part of it as the walls and the roof. There could be no question, though, of taking Sophronie along to Montreal. The idea of her living in town was quite unthinkable. Putting Big Sophronie into a house in Montreal would have been like trying to squeeze in the huge range from her kitchen or Jess the mare. My mother had made up her mind, however, that if Big Sophronie simply couldn't face the idea of separation, she would take her along anyway. After all she wouldn't be any more out of place in a town house than the drawing-room furniture. But, as it happened, neither the old servant nor the drawing-room furniture were destined to make the move.

One morning, at an hour when my mother could count on finding Sophronie alone in her kitchen, she went to have a talk with her. They sat on either side of the big table and the talk lasted a long time. The older woman sat knitting in her rocking-chair, but from time to time she got up to have a look at the dinner that was "on the stove." My mother went on talking, explaining just what had happened and that we had to leave and that everything would be sold. Sophronie said nothing; she just listened. When she had finished telling her the whole story, Mother took the old woman's hands in hers and added: "The house we are going to live in in Montreal isn't at all like this one, and everything there will be quite different from what you have known all your life. Still, if you want to come with me, I shall be only too happy. At your time of life, though, Sophronie, it's time you thought of taking a rest. You could go and live down in the village with your daughter and Godefroy or else go and stay in the convent with the Sisters of Providence. Whatever you decide to do, I shall always go on paying you what you are getting now. It will be for you to make up your mind. . . ."

Out of all that had been said, only one thing was clear to the old woman, and that was that they must part. For, from the start, she quite ruled out the possibility of going to live in town. She found the very idea as terrifying as if my mother had suggested they go up in a balloon or take a trip down to hell. The thought that we would have to go through such an experience appalled her.

The next few weeks were spent preparing for the move, and Sophronie was kept busy helping my mother and my sisters with the trunks and packing-cases. Often it happened that Old Sophronie's fingers and my mother's met while they were folding sheets or towels together, or wrapping up the kitchen utensils. The two women would then exchange a sad glance; there was no need for words to express their feelings.

My parents had to decide what furniture should be left behind and what was suitable for use in our new home in town. There were several sets of furniture in the old house, all with different origins. Sometimes my parents made up their minds to take along something for purely sentimental reasons; at other times, their choice was guided by the fact that a certain chair was comfortable to sit in. My mother was particularly set on the big sideboard in the dining-room because it could hold all the family porcelain and china. When this monumental piece reached the house in town it couldn't be got into the new dining-room and had to be left standing out in the hall. My father insisted on taking along an old Louis XVI chest-of-drawers with silver handles that had come down to him from his great-grandfather. During the move this ancient relic collapsed in the van and arrived in pieces. A cabinet-maker managed to put it together again and reinforced the poor old wooden frame with steel strips. My parents also took along to their new home all their bedroom furniture, which was really extraordinarily ugly. This included a huge bed made of black walnut and carved with wreaths and pendants, bedside tables to match, and two commodes with mysterious little compartments for chamber-pots. The drawing-room furniture was to stay behind in L'Assomption, for the authorities of the College had decided to buy it for the Bishop's parlour.

The two Sophronies and Godefroy were told by my parents that they could select anything in the house in the way of furniture or utensils that they might need for their new home down in the village. My father had found Godefroy a good job; he was to go and work for the Abbé Dorval. Godefroy was what in those days was still called a "hired man." This was an expression that went back to very early days in the history of the colony. In Louis XIV's reign, the habitants and seigneurs used to pay men's passages out from France if they undertook in return to work on their farms for five years. Young women were brought out to New France under the same system and were known as "hired girls." When I was a boy, people always spoke of hired men and hired girls, never of servants.

Even after the furniture question had been settled, there were a lot of things left in the house that nobody seemed to want, so my parents decided to have an auction sale.

A sale in that part of the country was always announced by the beadle on the steps of the church after High Mass on Sundays, and our auction was advertised in the same way. Then everything inside the old house that had to be sold was stacked on the gallery or in the yard or in the garden. The walks were lined with pieces of furniture, and all sorts of extraordinary objects were exposed to the full light of day for the first time. On the lawn itself were scattered the wooden chairs from the kitchen, two sitz-baths, a set of copper pots and pans, a number of four-poster beds, chandeliers and candelabra together with great piles of plates and dishes. Hervé and I, followed by the dogs, darted about among all this while Godefroy shouted: "You young devils, you'll bust everything and there's enough damage done around here the way it is." To be quite candid, it all did look rather the worse for wear, as most of it dated from the days of Uncle Saint-Ours, Uncle Viger and the seigneuresse. Even the commode was there, rearing up in august fashion among the spring flowers in the middle of one of the garden beds.

The junk from the attic was the weirdest of all. My mother had often remarked, "We'll have to clear out the attic," when she was doing the spring-cleaning. But the job had never been taken in hand. My sisters and brothers and I knew much better than my parents just what this storehouse of cast-off articles contained. It had provided us with an inexhaustible profusion of accessories for our games and theatricals, so it had few mysteries for us. But when all this was exposed to the public view, it did look rather odd. Grown-ups often fail to realize the secret uses to which children can put worn-out objects of every sort, old clothes, or broken-down furniture. When I gazed at the huge pile of old bits of furniture, "beaver" hats, tattered moccasins and splintered toboggans, the last-named once fashioned by Godefroy in a corner of the yard, I was actually looking at my favourite toys for the last time. There was the musket, complete with ramrod, which I had used to fight off Indians, the frock-coat with the moth-eaten collar that Hervé had dressed up in when he played priest and said the masses that I attended with Pipo, Porthos and the cats. And when it had all been sold to the highest bidder, and carted away by people who doubtless thought they had a use for all these things, my brother and I found ourselves deprived of all the best stage-properties for the dreams which we had acted out. The sale of the contents of the attic wiped out at one stroke my glorious career as a warrior and Hervé's as a priest.

The house stood empty at last. The auction had lasted a whole day. It was attended by people from the village, from neighbouring farms, from St. Sulpice and Repentigny, and when they drove off, nothing remained behind. The four-poster beds, the crockery, the big table from the kitchen, the saddles and sets of harness from the stable all found buyers. Carts and carriages rumbled off fully loaded. The auctioneer presided on the back veranda. His assistants fetched up the various items on display in the garden and held them up so that the crowd in the yard could see them. "Four bits for the bed . . . one buck . . . two . . . three bucks." Buyers shouted out their figures and bid keenly against one another. The bids would go up and up until finally a couple emerged from the throng carrying off something they had bought as if it were a trophy. By evening the whole garden had been trampled flat and the paths were almost obliterated, but the strange collection of objects, which for a time had turned the whole place into a curiosity shop, had disappeared.

Three vans had been standing in front of the house all day long. My father and Godefroy supervised the loading of the furniture and packing-cases which we were going to take to town with us. So the house was emptied of its contents in two directions at once. I was just a spectator and spent my time running backwards and forwards from the garden to the shed, making the dogs bark so that they drowned out the voices of the auctioneer and the bidders. When the time had come for us to leave, my father called me. The vans with our belongings were due to start for Montreal. The dogs were to make the trip with them, for there was a yard behind the house in town where we were going to live. There would be room there for Pipo and Porthos. My father felt that if we could keep the dogs we wouldn't miss the other animals so much. What he hated most was having to sell the two horses, but he watched them led away by the habitant who had bought them. He wouldn't let himself get sentimental about it and, above all, he wouldn't let anyone else see what he really felt, so he stalked back into the house with the remark, "They've got plenty of street-cars in town."

Now it was really time to leave. My sister Henriette helped me on with my overcoat. Hervé, who was never any trouble, was already sitting quietly in the carriage that was to take us to the station. He had one of the cats in his lap and I was supposed to take charge of another one—my favourite cat called Hang. But Hang was nowhere to be found. I went through all the rooms calling him by name. My voice echoed strangely in those empty spaces. I could hardly recognize the house any more; it seemed completely changed. I opened one door after another, but there was nothing except emptiness behind them. I went upstairs and ran down the hallway calling Hang and looking into every room in turn. I stopped suddenly for a panicky moment in the last one of all—the room on the west side of the house. I was in "the room," the one where people were sick and where people died. It was just as empty as all the others, but in one of the panes of the big window I caught sight of the vague outline of a face staring at me—doubtless a reflection of my own face in the opaque, bluish glass. It was just twilight and I suddenly felt frightened and rushed away without once looking back.

I ran right down to the kitchen. There was Hang under the stove. I picked him up in my arms and carried him out. The kitchen too was empty, deserted, abandoned. Once this huge room had been cheerful and cosy; now there was nothing left of all that. It already had a different smell. With the big table in the middle gone, it looked a vast place. The wooden arm-chairs had vanished and so had the cupboards and side-boards. Even the floor had been stripped of its *catalogne* carpets. In the whole kitchen the only thing remaining was the squat, black stove, but it too was cold and lifeless. For the first time in countless years no flames danced in its great belly or reddened its iron flanks. Missing from its usual place at the back, near the stove-pipe, was the coffee-pot, which always used to give off such a fragrant and potent aroma. Stripped of everything, this cold, silent stove was just so much old iron. The cat I hugged in my arms stared with puzzled eyes at this monster which it had always known as a source of heat and food and roaring sounds and which it must have venerated as a kind of household god. And now the god was dead.

I could hear them calling me. The carriage out in front of the porch was piled high with suitcases. My sisters had already climbed in and were sitting next to Hervé. My father gave Godefroy his final instructions and Mother was just about to get into the carriage when she seemed to hesitate, as if she couldn't bring herself to do it. Old Sophronie loomed up very tall in the background, holding a handbag; there were tears in her eyes and she couldn't utter a word. I ran over to her and threw myself into her arms. That made Hang the cat panic, because he felt himself being squashed between my arms and Sophronie's bosom, so he began to mew and struggle. The old servant gave me the handbag to take with me. It contained Mother's jewellery and, clutching it, I climbed up on to the seat.

My mother and the old servant parted with a kiss and a prolonged embrace. That kiss marked a moment in their lives when they both said good-bye to a happy life which had now ended.

As it happened, my mother and Sophronie did see each other again on several occasions later on. Up until the time of the old servant's death, Mother used to visit her at regular intervals, taking the train to L'Assomption a couple of times a year for that purpose. Sophronie lived with Godefroy and Little Sophronie in a clapboard house in the village. The three of them were always delighted by Mother's visits, but Big Sophronie was the most deeply moved on such occasions. Mother used to spend the whole day with them, and they would sit together in the combined living-room and kitchen of the little house, talking interminably about people and events from the past. Just for the space of a few hours they managed to recapture something of their former existence. Mother forgot all about her husband and children and her new home and her new life in Montreal. For the time being she was just a young girl again. The past and all its dead years slipped away from her and, when Mother looked at Sophronie, the old servant would grasp her hand and exclaim, "Mademoiselle, do you remember when. . . ."

These visits had a bitter-sweet quality for my mother. They reminded her all too poignantly that her youth lay behind her, and for a week or so after one of those trips there would be a sad, thoughtful look in her eyes. My father used to notice it and would do his best to distract her in order to make her forget all the old associations stirred up in her memory by seeing the old servant. He would generally take her out to the theatre.

Sometimes my mother took my sisters along with her on these visits to L'Assomption and, on one occasion, I was allowed to go along too.

I loved the train trip, for I was quite the big city boy by this time and liked speed and noise and the busy streets in the St. Louis de France district where we lived. By contrast, the village streets in L'Assomption seemed terribly quiet and dead. The old stone houses and the yellow-painted wooden ones seemed to me rather like toys. In a way it was all perfectly familiar and yet somehow quite strange. Things looked different and not as I remembered them. The church seemed small and the houses quite low. Even Sophronie looked older than I had imagined she would.

Sophronie and Godefroy lived out their completely uneventful lives in their little blue-painted house at the end of the village. Godefroy worked for the parish priest and made a habit of dropping in at "the major's place" on his way home every evening. This was the name they gave a tavern kept by an old Scotsman who made his living selling gin and whiskey by the drink. The tavern had an odd-looking, wooden figure perched above the door. This was a carving of a soldier who had fought in the war against the Americans in 1812, one of those who took part in the victory over General Hampton. It was nicknamed "the major." Little Sophronie had become very well-known indeed among the ladies of L'Assomption because of the quality of her needlework. She had always been particularly good at it, and now her sewing-machine occupied one corner of the room, near the window, and there were paper patterns and fashion magazines scattered on the centre table. At the back of the room towered a shiny, new stove. Old Sophronie used it for preparing those succulent dishes of hers that always smelled so good. The little seamstress' customers tried on their new party clothes in an odour of simmering stews and, when they shook out their long, panelled dresses, or unfolded the blouses they wore under their short, tight jackets, they must have been greeted with many a reminiscent whiff of stewed pigs' trotters or head-cheese.

When Big Sophronie wasn't fussing over her stove, she spent her time sitting in her rocking-chair, with a cat curled up in her lap, gazing out into the street where nothing ever happened.

I spent one whole day in Sophronie's little house. As we only had those few hours to spare, all the pleasures we used to enjoy in the past had to be crammed together within their span. I was showered generously with the gifts the old servant was able to dispense: the favourite dishes she alone knew how to cook, the exciting stories she had not forgotten how to tell.

Dinner at noon was served on the centre table, after the patterns and the sewing had been cleared away. Because of our visit, Godefroy came home earlier than usual. He seemed to have grown older too, like the two Sophronies, and had begun to be a bit stooped. He had always been thin but now he looked thinner and his big nose stood out even more prominently than before. He kissed Mother's hands and lifted me up in his arms to give me a big hug. I noticed his clothes still smelled of stables and gardens. Just in our honour, he had had a shave, as if it were Sunday. Sophronie had cooked us a wonderful dinner and I ate so much Mother became quite alarmed. But we never stopped talking, and that was a great help to digestion. Every now and then, however, a sort of sadness fell, whenever anybody mentioned some happy event in the past. Godefroy gave us all

the latest news about Jess and Tiger; he went to see them sometimes
at the farm of the habitant who had bought them. I, for my part,
talked about the dogs and Hang the cat, who had managed to get
accustomed to life in their back yard in town and even to running
about the streets, in spite of all the carriages and bicycles and street-
cars. Sophronie just couldn't see how we managed to go on living in
such a place and how we avoided being killed several times a day.
Nobody mentioned the manor-house.

We knew it wasn't standing empty any more and that there were
other people in it. It hurt my mother to think of strangers taking over
her house and to realize that though the dining-room, the living-
room, the kitchen and the upstairs bedrooms still existed, they were
used by other people. She preferred to imagine that the old house had
vanished and had somehow ceased to exist from the day she had
left it.

Towards the end of the afternoon, as there were still two hours to
while away before we had to start for the station, Sophronie and my
mother and I went out for a stroll. It was October and the pungent
tang of the countryside hung heavy in the village streets. We passed
the church and the garden of the convent of the Sisters of Providence,
where groups of old, retired priests sat on straw-bottomed chairs
chatting in low voices. Some of them strolled along the walks in
twos. Beyond the square, in front of the church, was the wooden
bridge crossing the little river, that flowed between narrow banks
overgrown with reeds and tall grasses. There was a carriage driving
across the bridge and the horses' hooves echoed against its planked
flooring. I could just see the two brick houses of the Faribaults
peeping through the screen of trees on the other bank of the river.

I recognized every single house in the village and knew just what
people lived behind those blank, silent walls. L'Assomption was a
very old village indeed and its houses, whether of stone or wood,
were all ancient. Here and there a few brick houses with "galleries"
around them introduced a touch of modernity and signified wealth
more recently acquired. In the gardens were round plots and rec-
tangular vegetable beds separated by paths bordered with white-
washed stones.

We were out in the open country now, walking along the highway.
My mother and Sophronie were deep in conversation and didn't look
up to see where they were. I ran back and forth and was sometimes
ahead of them and sometimes behind. There were so many things

that interested me: a peculiar-shaped tree, a crow perched on a fence-rail, the harsh croaking of the frogs in the weeds along the river. I was making contact again with things I had forgotten. Then Mother stopped suddenly.

Off in the distance, a line of tall trees blocked the horizon. You could just make out the wavy line of their topmost branches and catch a glimpse of a gable and a tall chimney. I realized these were the elm trees in the drive and the roof of the manor-house.

"Let's go back now," said Mother, and she turned round sharply.

We retraced our steps and had to walk fast to keep up with my mother. She had fallen silent and Sophronie had taken her arm. I started running up and down the road again and several times I turned round to look at the line of trees now fading out into the light autumn mist. But my mother never once looked back.

One winter Sophronie died. She was a very old woman by this time and so crippled by age she could hardly move from the rocking-chair where she dozed all day long. She was overjoyed by my mother's last visit, as she had been by all the others, and she managed to stand in front of the stove for a whole hour preparing one of Mademoiselle's favourite dishes: a bread-pudding with maple syrup. But the effort she made cost her dear. When Mother arrived by train at eleven in the morning she found the old servant lying pale and inert in her rocking-chair. What struck my mother most about the old woman's condition was that she had got so very thin. Sophronie hardly ate anything at all by that time. It was a sure sign that life was ebbing away from her. Eating and coaxing other people to eat had been her main preoccupation all her days. Now that the old woman had lost her own appetite and the physical strength to cook food for others, there was really no point in her going on living any longer. When my mother got home, she told us poor Sophronie would soon be leaving us.

The news of her death reached us by telephone. It was in the closing years of the nineteenth century that the telephone first came into use as the principal medium for announcing bad news. Thanks to this instrument, which was now being installed in most people's homes in Montreal, "subscribers" got their disagreeable news and were informed of deaths and other calamities with a minimum of delay. It was really a great convenience to have stuck away in some odd corner of the house a little box, complete with cord and bell, that could bring sudden grief and tears to the whole household. When my father answered the telephone on that occasion it was to hear Gode-froy's voice at the other end of the line. In spite of the nasal squawk-ings, he managed to make out what Godefroy was trying to say. Sophronie had died during the night.

For her, sleep and death had quietly merged. She hadn't suffered any pain and didn't even know she was dying. The old woman's affectionate and uncomplicated soul was whisked away to the pre-sence of her Creator without forewarning, but Sophronie is unlikely to have been greatly disconcerted; at most she was probably mildly surprised. She had always known perfectly well that she would have to go through the great adventure that all human beings must share. I like to think that the Lord had the compassion to show himself to his servant as she had always visualized Him, that is to say with long curly hair and beard, with blue eyes, and with his pierced and wounded hands pointing to his heart, crowned with flame, and worn outside the folds of his seamless robe.

My parents were present at Sophronie's funeral. They wore black for the occasion and Mother stayed in mourning for several days after they got back. She stopped wearing it finally because she didn't want to sadden us by reminding us of what had happened. But, for all that, none of us ever forgot Sophronie. For many years after her death, one or other of us would recall the traits that had so endeared her to us all and this kept alive the memory of a woman whose heart had overflowed with tenderness and true poetry.

After Sophronie's funeral, my parents never set eyes on L'Assomp-tion again. She had been the last link that bound them to that parti-cular place. We still sometimes spoke of the manor-house and of the life we used to lead there, but it had all become rather hazy and merged into a distant past that was gradually blotted out. Memories in their sharp, detailed outline became vaguer and vaguer until a whole period of our lives could be summed up in a single image: the manor-house. This phrase retained a special significance for all of us and always conjured up memories of the past. We only uttered it within the family circle, never before strangers. It was a sort of pass-word used by my parents and my brothers and sisters and myself, a secret incantation used as a means to return to a place we alone knew and where no one else had either the right or the power to penetrate.

But even this magic phrase finally dropped out of use among us. It gradually ceased to have any particular meaning, and so the words were spoken more and more rarely. They had lost their magic. Our new way of life had by now entirely enveloped the old one, with a complete new set of habits and familiar objects. The phrase had been the symbol of the old life; it died on our lips because the period it represented was now completely effaced. It was uttered for the last time the day we learned that the manor-house itself had disappeared forever.

One night the old house caught fire and burned to the ground. Nothing was left but crumbling walls of blackened stone. The drive-way lined with age-old elms now led only to a heap of ruins.

My father heard the news several days before he plucked up enough courage to tell us about it. He was particularly afraid that my mother might be very upset. So when he finally decided to tell us of the catastrophe the ashes of the house were cold and dead and already scattered by the winds. The kitchen where I spent so many long evenings with the two Sophronies and Sambo and Godefroy and Jacques, the living-room where my mother had so often sat dreaming beside the fireplace, the drawing-room, and the bedroom where we children had all been born had vanished.

My mother did not appear to be particularly upset by the news. The fact is that, as far as she was concerned, the manor-house ceased to exist the day she left it. The knowledge it had been blotted out somehow gave her a feeling of security. From now on she could safely return to it in her imagination and refashion it as we had once known and loved it. No alien presence could banish her from it any longer. The home of her childhood days, and of ours, the house where she had lived as a loving young wife and as a mother sur-rounded by a brood of children she adored, was now forever safe from destruction, enshrined in her thoughts and in her dreams.